TAKE BACK THE LAND

Inspiring a New Generation to Lead America

RICK BOYER

Dedicated to the memory of Chris Klicka, my best friend and a mighty warrior for Christ. Chris, we were going to write this book together but the Lord had other plans. I promised you I'd finish it and I promise I'll keep up the fight.

First printing: September 2011

Copyright © 2011 by Rick Boyer. All rights reserved. No part of this book may be used or reproduced in any manner whatsoever without written permission of the publisher, except in the case of brief quotations in articles and reviews. For information write:

Master Books®, P.O. Box 726, Green Forest, AR 72638
Master Books® is a division of the New Leaf Publishing Group, Inc.

ISBN: 978-0-89051-619-5
Library of Congress Number: 2011936603

Cover by Heidi Rohr

Unless otherwise noted, Scripture quotations are from the New American Standard version of the Bible.

Scripture taken from the NEW AMERICAN STANDARD BIBLE®, Copyright © 1960,1962,1963,1968,1971,1972,1973,1975,1977,1995 by The Lockman Foundation. Used by permission.

Scripture taken from the New King James Version. Copyright © 1982 by Thomas Nelson, Inc. Used by permission. All rights reserved.

Please consider requesting that a copy of this volume be purchased by your local library system.

Printed in the United States of America

Please visit our website for other great titles:
www.masterbooks.net

For information regarding author interviews,
please contact the publicity department at (870) 438-5288

Master
Books®
A Division of New Leaf Publishing Group
www.masterbooks.net

Contents

Introduction

This is a book for young people. It was written because I believe young people are important and that they have a huge part in God's plan for the future of America and the Church. In fact, you *are* the future. And a big part of the present, too.

I'm writing to homeschooled young people in particular, and for two reasons. The first is that homeschooling is my mission. That's where God has put me. My passion is the Christian family, and homeschooling is the purest form of it. The second reason is this: I believe that home education is producing, and will produce, the future leaders of our culture. I believe that you will lead America into decades of revival and national reformation. If you don't, there is little hope for our country. A lot depends on you.

If you're a young person who was not homeschooled, this book is still for you. Just ignore the places where I assume that all my readers are homeschoolers. The message is still intended for you. I hope that one day you will consider teaching your own kids at home, but for now come on along for the ride. If you're a believer in Jesus Christ, your calling is to change the world around you, regardless of your educational background.

I hope your parents will read this book, too. They are critical to God's plan for your life, and it's important that you and they are singing on the same page as you look toward His life mission for you. But I have already written several books for homeschooling parents and there are lots of good books written for them by others. I don't know of any book written especially for their sons and daughters, and there is a lot I want to say to you.

Actually, this book grew out of a speech I made to a group of young people. It was a graduation speech I presented at the Iowa statewide homeschool commencement service in May 2008. On that sunny Saturday afternoon, I told 106 bright, beaming young men and women some of the things I'm going to tell you in this book. I gave them a challenge — a challenge to worship a big God and attempt big things for Him because that is our purpose in life.

My talk got a standing ovation that day (which doesn't happen *every* single time I speak). Of course the audience's appreciation is always heartwarming to a public speaker. But the thing that blessed me the most was the fact that it was the graduates themselves who were on their feet first. They had liked what I said.

As I reflected later on the speech and the grads' response, it came to me with jolting clarity that those grads weren't hailing a brilliant speech. They weren't responding to eloquence or genius or exceptional good looks (in fact, I'm pretty sure about that last one). They were simply thanking me for a high compliment.

There are, after all, different kinds of commencement addresses. Some are apologies. "Here's the world we're leaving you, lots of luck. Our generation has messed it up thoroughly and it's a pretty rotten place, so . . . hope you can do better." Other graduates hear speeches full of flattery. "Oh, you young folks are so wonderful. Those video games have just made paragons of virtue out of you. We know you'll go far."

But I simply offered them a challenge: Grow up. Now. Get busy. Take responsibility to change this world for God, because that's exactly what He expects you to do.

With all my heart I believe that those young people were just saying thank you. Thank you for believing that our lives matter. Thank you for saying that we *must* change the world, because that tells us that you believe we *can* change the world. Thank you for reminding us that God has big plans for us and that this ceremony marks not the end of our youth, but the first day of the rest of our lives. And that God wants to make those lives great.

In fact, I was a little tough on those young men and women. I communicated very high expectations and allowed for no excuses. But looking back, I think that was exactly what they turned on to. You guys really don't want life to be easy, you want it to be worthy. That's the kind of life I will offer you in this book.

Pioneer missionary William Carey once said, "Attempt great things *for* God. Expect great things *from* God."

My young friend, God is calling you to greatness.

No excuses.

Chapter 1

DON'T WASTE YOUR YOUTH

I wrote this book to develop and broaden the challenge I gave to those homeschool graduates in Iowa. Those young people made a lifelong impression on me with their excitement about an idea: the idea that their generation is responsible for the future of America. They seemed eager to do their part and excited about the prospect of being involved in something bigger than themselves, something great that they could do for the glory of God.

I hope you're excited about that prospect, too. Because it is very real. Our culture is in desperate shape, and my generation has been praying for national revival for many years. I believe that your generation is the answer to our prayers.

Maybe the first thing you'll have to do is reject the pop culture's expectations for young people. When I say young people — at least for the purpose of this book — I mean people of the age usually associated with middle school, high school, and college, maybe 12 through the middle twenties. If I meant someone younger, I might use the word child or children. If you are through puberty, I consider you an adult. A young adult, a less experienced adult, but absolutely an adult, nevertheless.

That's radically different from the pop culture model, which assumes that at least through your teen years you will be goofy, silly, unable to handle responsibility, and only interested in things of little importance. You won't care much about grown-up issues like politics, economics, faith, and community service. You'll want to spend all your time hanging out at the mall, flirting, wasting money, gabbing on Facebook, watching TV, and listening to music. You'll be looking for fun, not achievement.

I say that's hogwash. I know any number of young folks, including my own sons and daughters, who are living a different way. They are doing real things in the real world, facing real challenges and meeting real needs. And they're loving it.

So let's cut to the chase. I'm an old guy writing to young men and women. I'm here to tell you that the world is in a mess and it's your job to change it, beginning with the culture you grew up in. I will address you as adults and expect you to consider what I say and — agree or disagree — respond as adults. I respect you that much and I hope you respect yourselves. After all, God made you — very specifically (see Psalm 139) — and He does not make junk.

I will make no attempt in this book to be cool. I won't bother to use the contemporary teen lingo because I know you're just as capable of understanding plain English as your parents are. I don't normally use the phrase "like, totally" so I won't use it here. And I will make no effort to remember to address you as "dude." If you attend one of our Take Back the Land conferences, you won't see me dressed in shredded jeans and sneakers, trying to pretend I'm up on the latest youth fashions and fads. I'll be in a suit and tie. Why? Because I love a choke string around my neck? No. I hate ties and never wear one to the office. It's because I respect you and don't consider you a group of dumb kids. I figure I'm talking to future presidents, Supreme Court justices, pastors, CEOs, business owners, authors, etc., so I dress appropriately. I would wear a suit if I was invited to the White House, so I'm going to wear a suit when I talk to you at a conference. You are somebody and I'm going to show you respect.

I'm also not going to knock myself out to convince you of how understanding I am. I'm not going to try to sound "relevant," whatever that worn-out term is supposed to mean. What's really relevant in life is not what's relevant to the bogus youth subculture of the last several decades (yes, believe it or not, youth culture is not that new) but what's relevant to the eternal Word of God and the lessons of several thousand years of human experience. What's really relevant to life is a lot of very old-fashioned values that speak of things like decency and respect and diligence and wisdom and responsibility. The kind of things that my parents tried to teach me, and which I was too cool to pay much attention to.

I trust you're smarter than I was at your age. But if you've bought the tired notion that you're coming of age in a new era of history that requires different music, different dialect, different clothes, etc., forget it. That's what my generation thought 40 years ago. There's really nothing new under the sun. Nearly everything that is pawned off on each new generation of young people is driven by mass marketing. And it's not marketing done by young people, either.

So don't write off my ideas because I'm old and you think I can't understand you. I understand enough. I've been young. I've lived with a lot of young people, too, watching several of my 14 children who are now in their thirties, right from the get-go. And to the best of my knowledge hormones haven't changed, peer pressure hasn't changed, and zits haven't changed. You'll get much better mileage if you stop worrying about whether I understand you and start trying to understand me. I'm four decades past high school and this ain't my first rodeo. If you would just learn from all the mistakes I've made you'd hardly have to make any of your own.

So don't look for older people to understand you. Instead, apply yourself to understanding them. Watch them, get to know them, learn all you can from their experience, both positive and negative. A lot of them would be delighted to share the wealth of their many years of wisdom with a young person who has sense enough to want to hear it.

Most people have low expectations of young people these days. A symptom of that attitude is the fact that most churches hire 20-somethings as youth ministers. We assume that young folks don't have an adult level of interest in spiritual things, nor an adult attention span. They can't handle adult instruction in Christian living; they have to be entertained constantly. If you send them on a short-term missions trip, make sure it's near a beach. They can do some useful work, but they have to spend at least half of each day swimming. They need their own brand of music; songs that have stood the test of time for centuries are over their young heads. The youth director has to know the latest teen lingo and is even cooler if he sports a couple of tattoos. If you want to reach young people you have to come "down to their level."

Aren't you a little insulted by the assumption that your "level" is "down"? I think all that is ridiculous, so I won't be attempting to come down to anybody's level. I was young once, and I wasted those years doing the same stupid, empty things so many people expect you to do now. It makes me sick to look back and see what I cheated myself out of. So no, I won't be coming down to your level. I'm inviting you to come up to mine.

Come on up. Come on and join us. The greatest adventure known to man is waiting for you; it's the cause of being a soldier for Jesus Christ. Fighting His battles for truth, righteousness, and the salvation of men. In our country it's also the battle for human freedom, as an army of Christian patriots rise up once again, as in 1776, to stand for the freedom of "we the people."

If you haven't done so yet, it's time to graduate from the "youth group" mentality. Stop thinking of yourself as a second-class citizen in the Church and community just because you're under voting age. Consider yourself a full-fledged member of the Body of Christ and an American citizen. Depending on your exact age, there may be some privileges you can't yet take advantage of. That's fine; to everything there is a season (see Ecclesiastes 3), and your time will come for full participation. But there is much you can do now. You can make a huge difference if you will reject the labels society tries to paste on the young and get on about the business of serving God and the other people around you.

Okay, so I'm inviting you to start living the adult life now. What do I mean by that? What does it look like to be an adult rather than a "teenager" or an "adolescent"? Well, here are some of the marks of adult character as I see it.

An adult has his own real relationship with God. He doesn't expect to enter heaven on his parents' faith. He has repented of his sins, accepted salvation through the blood of Christ, and walks daily in fellowship with God through prayer and the reading and study of the Scriptures. He understands that he is responsible to grow spiritually for the rest of his life.

An adult takes responsibility for his own actions. He does what he should do, regardless of whether he's being supervised or not. He doesn't go around inventing excuses for underperformance or complaining about how bad conditions are. He does what he can to make conditions better and to make the most of things as they are. He admits it when he's been wrong.

An adult has decided to be a giver rather than a taker. Usually by the end of puberty, this decision has been made and it is evident to others. An adult sees himself as more of a producer than a consumer. This is simply the natural manifestation of the choice to do as Jesus commanded, to serve rather than be served. This attitude affects every major decision in life. An adult is not shackled with the constant concern of "What's in it for me?" This also affects our outlook as we decide how to spend our time. Rather than thinking, *What would be a fun way to spend tomorrow?* he thinks, *What would be a worthwhile way to spend tomorrow?* The underlying question for an adult is, "How can I spend tomorrow so that I will look back on it with thankfulness rather than regret?" An adult knows that his time on earth is limited and he wants to spend it on things that matter.

An adult lives with a conscious sense of duty. Duty is a word that's not used very often anymore, and it's a shame. It's related to the idea of being a giver rather than a taker, and it's pretty much the opposite of the popular idea of looking out for Number One. Duty means taking responsibility for the world around you, looking more to your responsibilities than to your rights, whether as a family member, a friend, an employee/employer, or a citizen. As Americans, we have wonderful rights protected by law. Unfortunately, we live in a selfish time when many Americans are majoring on their rights and minoring on their responsibilities. Everybody wants his "entitlements" but few want to know what their duties as citizens are. That's a very dangerous state of affairs, because tyrants often rise to positions of power in government by promising people more entitlements and less responsibility.

A duty-conscious person is looking for ways to be helpful in his family, his church, his employment, his community, and his country. Dutiful people volunteer for extra housework, look for ways to make their employers and employees more successful, join the rescue squad, and work the polls on election day. Contrast this to people who spend all their free time watching TV and playing Xbox.

Now please don't hear what I'm not saying. I'm not saying that pleasure is evil or that there is no place in life for rest and recreation. I'm talking priorities. Everybody needs some rest and some fun. But we need to understand that the best rest comes after we've worked hard enough to do somebody some good. The best fun is found in the good times we have, knowing that we've done our duty and it's time now for some well-deserved play.

In modern American culture we have our priorities backward. We work as much as we have to in order to survive. But we're usually much more excited about our fun than about the contribution we're making to the rest of the world. That's the reason the entertainment industry is one of the very biggest businesses in the country. We worship pleasure.

Let me illustrate. Do you know who Brett Favre is? Sure. He plays football. Tiger Woods? He plays golf. Mick Jagger? He plays music. Sort of. Tom Cruise? He plays other people in movies. These people all *play* for a living, and we all know their names.

But do you know these names: Christian Barnard, Jonas Salk, Alexander Fleming?

Dr. Christian Barnard performed the first successful human heart transplant. Jonas Salk created the Salk vaccine that stopped the crippling plague of polio. Sir Alexander Fleming developed the antibiotic penicillin, saving millions of lives.

Now how many Americans know the names on the second list? How many teenagers have posters of those guys on their bedroom walls? Yet which of the two lists contains the names of the people who have contributed more to humanity? I think you see what I mean. We have become a nation that is more defined by our play than by our work. That's what happens when several successive generations seek their pleasure rather than their duty.

This fun-and-games society has conditioned many adults to take their childishness with them right into adulthood. It used to be the other way around. If we weren't so ignorant of our own history (partly because we spend our free time watching the tube instead of reading) we'd know that it wasn't so long ago that kids actually wanted to be adults. They didn't waste a lot of time in the process of growing up.

Our sixth president, John Quincy Adams, drilled with the Massachusetts militia during the Revolutionary War. He was 8 years old at the time. At 11, he served as secretary to his father, John Adams, who was the American envoy to France at the time. At 14, Congress appointed him secretary to America's envoy to Russia.

Thomas Edison, the inventor of the light bulb, didn't wait forever to grow up either. At 12, he was working on the Grand Trunk Railroad. He was also publishing a newspaper on a castoff printing press he had rebuilt himself. He printed it in the baggage car and then sold it to the passengers. His career on the railroad was cut short because some chemical experiments he was working on in his spare time caught the baggage car on fire.

David Farragut, the first admiral in the U.S. Navy went to sea as a midshipman when he was nine years old. Years later in the War of 1812, his ship fought with and captured a British warship. Farragut was given command of the prize and ordered to sail it from the west coast of South America all the way back to Boston. He was 12 years old at the time.

On another ship in another war, another young man distinguished himself. Calvin Graham, Seaman First Class, was a part of the crew of the USS *South Dakota* in World War II. In the naval battle of Guadalcanal, the ship was hit by Japanese artillery and caught fire. Graham was seriously wounded. Despite that, he not only took part in the fire control efforts but also rescued several wounded sailors who otherwise would have been burned to death. Graham was given a Purple Heart for his wounds, a Bronze Star for his heroism, and a discharge for lying. During his recovery it was discovered that he had falsified his enlistment papers. He was only 12 years old.

Benjamin Franklin — statesman, diplomat, scientist, philanthropist, and too many other titles to mention — went to school for only two years. Most of his remarkable education he took for himself in his limited spare time after working 12-hour days as a printer's apprentice. By the time he reached middle age he was one of the most successful and famous men in the English-speaking world. Much of his fame was due to the success of his *Poor Richard's Almanac*, but his publishing career started much earlier when, under a pen name, he anonymously slipped his articles under the newspaper editor's door in the middle of the night. He was in his mid-teens then.

All these guys lived a good while ago, but they don't have an exclusive claim to early achievement. Do an Internet search of the phrase *child prodigy* and you'll come up with more info than you care to read about kids who did adult things at very young ages. Early maturity was certainly much more common early in our history than it is now, but it's not because human nature is different now. Rather, it's the way children are being brought up.

You see, maturity and responsibility are two sides of the same coin. This whole book is my plea to you to take on responsibility in order to develop maturity and demonstrate maturity by taking on responsibility. People who take responsibility early grow up early. Some people, like me, don't really grow up until they get married because they manage to avoid responsibility during their teen years. It's not until they get married that they find themselves with responsibilities they can't wiggle out of. Then they tend to grow up pretty fast, if the marriage survives.

But a hundred years ago, young people routinely carried serious loads of responsibility long before marrying age. Most of the country lived on farms or in small towns. Everybody had their chickens, hogs, and cows for meat, eggs, and milk. Everybody had horses for transportation. Children grew up caring for younger children — the average family had seven — and a collection of animals who depended on their human benefactors for their very survival. Both kids and critters had to be taken care of in all kinds of weather, at various times of day or night, and whether it was convenient or not. Young people learned early in life that the world didn't revolve around them. And they learned they could handle it.

But the social engineers in and around government viewed all this self-sufficiency and independence with disapproval. Independent people think for themselves, which makes them hard to govern. They tend to think of the citizenry as the bosses and the elected officials as public servants. Independent types also tend to be self-employed, which limits the supply of candidates for assembly-line workers and labor union members. Not to mention the fact that these people tend to have close families in which values are passed down from generation to generation. That was unhandy for other social manipulators who were concerned with changing public opinion in favor of socialism or secularism or whatever "ism" they happened to believe in.

That's why the process of growing up changed so much in America in the last century. Lots of people wanted to control the rest of the population, so they had to make people childlike and irresponsible. Childhood had to be artificially extended so that the citizenry was easier to lead (and mislead). Friedrich Engels, early Communist leader and friend of Karl Marx, author of *The Communist Manifesto,* once said that if you could remove a people from their roots, they could be easily swayed to your point of view.[1] Of course, he meant persuaded to give up their freedom in exchange for socialism (communism).

Engels was right. The correctness of his statement now has a hundred years' worth of proof. That's about how long the statists (people who believe the government should control the citizens instead of vice versa) have been using compulsory school attendance to reduce the amount of time kids spend with their parents and siblings. The result has been less parental influence on kids, less loyalty of kids to parents, less bonding between brothers and sisters, less passing on of family values and traditions. There has been increasing peer dependency and a slowing of maturity as kids spend less time with adults and more time with people their own age. It's ironic that we adults put our kids into so many same-age activities and expect them to grow up. How can they, when we surround them with immature social models? A 13 year old already knows how to be a 13 year old.

Another way social engineers have segregated young people from the maturing influence of adults is through child labor laws. Starting around 1900, attempts were made to use the rough conditions in many workplaces to convince lawmakers to pass bills protecting young people from them. (You'll see this method in frequent use even today as we are constantly being sold the need for more government regulation — which, translated, means less personal freedom — for the sake of "protecting" somebody from something). The assumption is that kids and their parents are too dumb to decide how old a person should be when he starts working or what jobs are too dangerous for young people. The social engineers took advantage of the fact that there were some young people being abused in workplace situations to convince lawmakers that the problem was huge and required solutions on a national level. (Watch for this ploy as you educate yourself about the political system — a problem faced by a tiny minority will often be inflated to persuade legislators to pass laws affecting many millions of citizens, and for a totally different reason.)

It worked. It took a long time, but the statists have been so successful that most of the public now accepts as normal an American youth lifestyle that keeps kids locked up in schools for most of their productive hours and away from the challenging environment of real work. It also keeps them surrounded by people no more mature than they are themselves most of the time. The result? It's taking years longer to grow up than it did a century ago.

I heard a great illustration of this phenomenon in a speech by a career counselor. This guy was an older gentleman who had been in the business for probably 40 years. He said, "When I was starting out in the business, people who came to me for advice usually had a pretty good idea of where they wanted to go in life by about age

20. Now, it's more like age 30. I don't know exactly why that is, but it's a very clear pattern." Wow. He's saying that it's taking people 50 percent longer to decide on a career direction than it did just four decades ago.

I think I know why it is. We're not growing up because we're not hanging around with grown-up people, doing grown-up work, reading grown-up books, and thinking about grown-up issues. We're not getting out into the adult world while we're still young and finding out what's available to us and what we're suited for. What we find fulfillment in doing. We're spending our youth in an artificial environment instead of the real world of home, community, church, and workplace. We spend the most energetic, creative years of our lives separated from the business of the real world. No wonder it takes so long to find our place in it when we're finally turned loose.

Once I was looking through some old magazines and I came across a photo of a 14-year-old guy walking to school in the winter. He was wearing a coat and tie, an overcoat, and a style of hat that I think is called a fedora. (I'm not a hat guy, except for the John Deere cap I wear here at the farm.) The photo must have been taken around the 1930s or 40s. The thing that struck me about the boy was that he was dressed like an adult man. He must have looked just like his dad on his way to the office.

I've since noticed the same thing in many old photos. The little kids are dressed like little kids, the girls in ruffly dresses and the boys in knickers and long socks. But from about middle school age on up, they were dressed just like their parents. Kids used to want to look like adults.

I've now learned enough to know that back then kids wanted to act like adults, too. They wanted to be adults. They wanted to grow up and take their places in the real world. A creature called a teenager was unknown in the early 20th century. There were children and there were adults. Some of those adults were in their teen years, many still living in their parents' homes and under their authority, but carrying their own load of responsibility in the family and often in the family business or farm. There was no intermediate category called "teenager." You were a child or you were an adult.

Today, you can be a child, you can be an adult, or you can be a teenager. Sometimes we extend the pre-adult category to adolescent, which seems to include teenagers and 20-somethings who still aren't supporting themselves. In our culture, an adolescent seems to be defined as a human creature who has all the freedom of an adult to do what he pleases, but the light responsibility load of a child. Sounds like a pretty good deal. But all is not as it seems. One would think an "adolescent" has it made in the shade, but evidently it's not so. America leads the world in opportunity for adolescents, yet suicide is the third leading cause of death for Americans ages 15 through 24.[2] It appears that freedom from responsibility isn't all it's cracked up to be.

So I'm offering you a different way to go. I'm suggesting you just skip adolescence. Decide to grow up now and take responsibility for your life. Take responsibility to do all the good you can do in the world around you. That doesn't mean you're no longer under your parents' authority. It just means you're accepting responsibility for your actions. It means you're determined to amount to something, rather than playing your youth away. I believe you're up to the challenge. That's why I speak to you as an adult, rather than an adolescent.

Like, totally, dude.

Endnotes

1. http://www.onthewing.org/user/Edu_Dewey%20-%20Father%20of%20Modern%20Education.pdf.

2. http://en.wikipedia.org/wiki/Teenage_suicide_in_the_United_States.

Chapter 2:

THE JOSHUA GENERATION

It was home education advocate Mike Farris who coined the term "the Joshua Generation." He was referring to the young people who were and are being taught at home by the early homeschooling parents. By that he meant those of us who were homeschooling in the early days of the movement, the ones who fought the legal battles of the 1980s to establish our freedom to teach our kids as we saw fit. As Mike sees it, we older folks are the Moses generation. We all grew up in public school because the law said we had to be there. But there came a time when God led a few of us, now parents ourselves, to reject the world's system and teach our own children. We were like Moses. We led the movement out of the Egypt of our day, speaking allegorically of government school.

That was the beginning of a great movement. I personally think it was the beginning of a spiritual revival as the hearts of parents turned to their children and vice versa. It seems to me that that step, taking back responsibility for the training of our kids, was the first step in taking back an American culture that has drifted far from God and His standards.

But it was only the first step. Though today homeschooling is clearly legal almost everywhere in America, there are many cultural battles yet to be fought. My generation set you free from the Egyptian training that we were all subjected to, but our culture is far from reformed. It's your turn now.

You sons and daughters of the modern homeschooling movement really are the Joshua generation. Your parents got you out of Egypt, you're through the wilderness and at the River Jordan. The Promised Land is just on the other side. But there are enemies over there. You have battles ahead of you.

In my speech to the Iowa graduates, I spoke from Joshua chapter 1, using Mike's metaphor. If you'll stop and think about it, you'll see some interesting parallels between you and those second-generation Israelite refugees from slavery.

Canaan had been given to Abraham by God, to be a home to him and his descendants forever. But his children and grandchildren had gone to Egypt during a famine, where at first brother Joseph took care of them but they were eventually enslaved. During their absence from Canaan, pagans moved in and built strongholds in the land such as the cities of Jericho, Ai, Kiriath-arba, and a bunch of other unpronounceable places.

Then, more than four centuries after Israel left Canaan, Moses rose to leadership and led Israel out of bondage. After 40 years of wandering in the wilderness, Moses and nearly all of his generation

had died. God told Moses' servant Joshua to lead the new generation of Israelites back into the land that had once belonged to their
tribe and settle down.

One problem. They weren't going to be welcomed by the squatters, and some of those squatters were giants. The Moses generation
had led Israel out of slavery, but it was the Joshua generation that
was going to have to take back the land. One stronghold at a time.
It would be all-out war.

Now think for a minute about the nation you live in, the United
States of America. At the beginning of our national government,
we were the freest (is that a word?) people on the face of the earth.
We were also very Christian in our national philosophy, our common culture. Research has shown that around 95 percent of our
founding fathers were God-fearing evangelical Christians. This was
reflected in our community life, our laws, our schools, and our standards of behavior. Christians were in leadership in all the major areas of our culture. But very gradually we drifted away from biblical
truth. Christians began to abandon territory that was historically
ours. Eventually, we were dominated by the world's system.

Today, as you young people look at the culture around you and
try to envision your future place in it, you see enemy strongholds
across the river. They're not stone fortifications in places called Ai
and Jericho, they are spiritual strongholds in the family, in the
Church, in the government, in the courts, the media, the arts, etc.
They have been built over a period of many years as Christians have
gradually given ground before pagan philosophies. We've failed to
take a firm stand on biblical truth and have been edged out of many
places of influence.

Like Canaan of old, America was once considered the Promised
Land of the modern world. To a great extent it still is: the opportunities

for a better life that still remain cause millions of people to break immigration laws to get here. There doesn't seem to be any mass exodus to leave here and go to other countries. We're still reaping the benefits of freedom and prosperity that our godly forefathers sowed at the cost of their fortunes and their blood over two centuries ago. But things have gone a long way downhill. We're daily losing freedom to an increasingly oppressive government, and our prosperity is in danger of sinking in an ocean of national and personal debt.

That's where you come in. Yes, you.

Homeschooling parents are the modern Moses generation. They take students out of bondage to the public school system, which our increasingly secular government has used for over a century to weaken family loyalties and indoctrinate kids with secular values. Much of the decline of Christian influence in our society can be blamed on those schools. I know. I'm a survivor of them. But because of the courage of these moms and dads, young people have had a different walk through life. They've been taught to think a different way. And now it's your turn to show some courage.

Will you pay the price to take back the land?

Yes, your parents' generation won some battles. But that was on our side of the river. Your future lies on the other side. There are still enemy strongholds over there. They will either be conquered by your generation or they will grow in strength and re-enslave you and your children. Take a good look across the river and start planning your attack.

Satan has erected strongholds in family life. Forty percent of American children are born out of wedlock. We lead the world in divorce and teen suicide.

There are enemy strongholds in the Church. We've watered down God's message to avoid offending the world. We preach an "easy believism" gospel that majors on tolerance and says nearly nothing about repentance and the holiness of God. Our compromise has brought us only contempt from the world we are trying to reach.

There are strongholds in our government. Our legislators buy votes with money stolen from the voters to keep themselves in power. Our courts routinely rule against godly standards and exalt perversion. Unelected bureaucracies like the Environmental Protection Agency and the Internal Revenue Service trample upon citizens' rights.

There are strongholds in the media. A recent survey showed that two-thirds of media leaders believe it is important for them to impose their values on the American public. Needless to say, most of those values aren't God's values.

There are strongholds in the arts. Movies have gradually deadened our sensitivity to evil. Music has almost become a religion in itself, and most of what you hear is, shall we say, less than edifying. Television has become a moral cesspool. Even sculpture has degenerated, with unidentifiable "impressionistic" structures where statues of heroes used to stand.

There are several other cultural strongholds, but you get the point. Our formerly Christian nation has turned away from our old foundations and the culture is rotting. A lot of the public godlessness you see today was hidden away for shame when I was your age. Your parents' generation has begun to turn the tide and it's time for you to pick up the torch.

Now.

Home Education and Reformation in America

One reason I believe home education is the key to revival in our culture is that it is a rejection of the system that I blame in large part for our present apostasy, the "public" school system. That's a misnomer, of course. The schools are government schools. They're not public at all, except in the sense that the public pays the taxes that support them and suffers the consequences of their existence. The government controls what is taught in those schools, and the parents who are rearing the students and paying the taxes for the schools have almost no input. Their values are not respected and in fact are often undermined.

There was a time, early on in our history, when everybody would have laughed at the idea of compulsory school attendance. In the first place, it wasn't needed. There was homeschooling, tutoring, and lots of affordable private schools. Literacy was much higher at the time of the American Revolution than it is now (see John Taylor Gatto, *Dumbing Us Down*[1]). Schooling wasn't worshiped as the answer to all problems because people had been educating themselves quite adequately for generations with very little time spent in school.

More importantly, the *compulsory* nature of today's schooling would have seemed both weird and offensive. In the early days, when Americans could remember the struggle to become a free country, the idea of a law confining innocent people to government institutions for most of each day, five days a week, nine months of the year would not have been tolerated. It would have been seen for what it is: imprisonment of the innocent. Promoters of compulsory attendance pointed to the very small percentage of American children who were not being educated and used them as an argument for their agenda. Once again, the needs of a very few were used as leverage to infringe on the freedom of all.

Once compulsory attendance had become the law of the land (around the early 1900s), the public school system gave the government and those who had influence in government the opportunity to effectively brainwash a large percentage of the population. That's partly why public attitudes toward moral, economic, and political issues changed so radically over the last hundred years. The schoolroom provided a captive audience for various liberal idealogies, like atheism or homosexuality, to program their chosen worldview into vulnerable young minds. The pulpit, once the most influential voice in the nation, gradually lost influence to the point that it is almost ignored today. And with the Supreme Court decisions of the early 1960s that removed prayer and Bible reading from the public schools, biblical truth is virtually expelled from the classroom.

Oh my goodness, here I am writing a book for young people and I've lapsed into serious stuff like philosophy and politics! You're not interested in all that, right? You can't handle serious thinking, right?

Baloney. We continue.

I blame government education for a lot of the problems we have today, especially the erosion of our freedom. Our public schools produce just the kind of young people one would expect a government to want: passive, uncritical thinkers who are unlikely to start any revolutions; conditioned by long practice to do what they're told, moving in groups, with weak family loyalties and strong peer dependency.

Fill in the blank. Copy this off the blackboard. Sit still and be quiet. Don't question why we do it this way, just do it. Give us the answers we want or we will punish you. Know your place: mainstream, gifted, or LD. We will tell you what you're worth. We will tell you what to read. We will tell you what to think. We will drug you if you get out of hand. We will tell you what you need to learn.

We will tell you, by golly, when to go to the bathroom. You're not here to learn how to run your own life.

That's not the educational system that produced Washington, Jefferson, and Franklin. And no wonder. The government controls schooling now, and government wants worker bees, not revolutionaries. Followers, not leaders. Groupthinkers, not philosophers. People who go with the flow rather than rocking the boat.

Those early American boat rockers got a huge part of their education at home. Franklin, for instance, went to school for only two years, total. For the most part, he educated himself. Washington and Jefferson likewise got their educations outside the public schools. Washington went to the university at 13. At 14, Jefferson was running the family plantation, an orphan. In those days, people carried responsibility early and grew up early. Today, I see the same thing happening with homeschooled young people. They are more mature, they take responsibility, and they know how to think critically. They are preparing to lead America back to the spirit of the founders.

America, the greatest nation in the world, came about because some people were willing to risk everything to rock the boat. And I'm proud of your parents because they are the new patriots who are rocking it again. I'm also proud of you for reading a book like this. A lot of people your age are playing video games right now.

The boat needs a lot more rocking. And it's your turn.

Now let's go back to the Joshua allegory. Like the Promised Land, America was originally given to believers in the one true God. Evangelism of the natives was one of the main reasons the early colonists, including the Pilgrims, came here. A decade and a half later, when the Founders were establishing our national government, they looked to the Bible for principles on which to build it.

So it was Christianity that birthed America. The founders were not the agnostics and deists that you read about in the modern history texts. Even Franklin and Jefferson, often described as antagonistic to Christianity, were anything but. Franklin was a good friend of evangelist George Whitefield and encouraged church attendance while governor of Pennsylvania. He also supported many ministries with his own money. Jefferson, while president, decreed that the Bible and Watts' hymnal should be the main reading texts in the Washington, DC, public schools. While researching the signers of the Declaration of Independence for her book *For You They Signed,* my wife Marilyn discovered that nearly every one of those men left a clear testimony of his faith in Christ in a diary, letter, will, or some other document.

In colonial and revolutionary times and for a long time after that, the Bible was revered throughout America. Christian thought dominated home life, church life, community life, and political life. Everybody quoted the Bible, from government officials to newspaper editors. To be called a true Christian was the highest compliment one could receive, and to insult Christianity or treat God's name with anything less than reverence was considered an abomination. America was avowedly a Christian nation. Nobody questioned that. The Supreme Court didn't babble about "separation of church and state" (that phrase isn't even in the Constitution, by the way) in the early days, nor in fact until after World War II.

What I'm saying is that Christian philosophy was the standard for family, church, government, school, business, the media, and the arts. America was built primarily by Christians.

Sadly, Christians have largely abandoned these cultural institutions today. The family has deteriorated. Our government now tries to ban the Bible from the public discourse. Public schools are seminaries of humanism. The mainstream media is anti-God. The arts, supported in part by tax dollars, have in many cases become showcases of smut. Christianity, instead of leading society with its timeless truth, is being hounded into oblivion.

Why has this happened? Because Christians have abandoned the battlefield. We have let the enemy gain control of our major social institutions. We have ceased to preach the truth of God's Law. We have gotten lazy and the enemy has grown strong through our complacency. Now we're waking up and trying desperately to hold on to what little freedom we have left with which to serve the Lord. We've gone on the defensive and become the tail and not the head.

I say we need to fight back. And I don't believe we should circle the wagons and hang on to what's left. That wasn't Joshua's attitude. He wasn't content to squat on the bank of the Jordan and fortify against a possible attack from the other side. God had told him to "go over this Jordan, thou, and all this people, unto the land which I do give to them, even to the children of Israel" (Josh. 1:2; KJV), and that's what he did. He wasn't a defensive fighter. He had been called to conquer, and he intended to conquer.

Remember what Jesus said to Peter? "Thou art Peter [a stone], and upon this rock I will build my church; and the gates of hell shall not prevail against it" (Matt. 16:18; KJV). Now think about it. Are *gates* offensive in nature or defensive? Jesus wasn't warning Peter against Satan jerking a gate off hell's hinges and smacking the Church over the head with it. He was telling His disciples He expected offensive warfare out of them. That's His approach.

Gates are only useful for two things: keeping attackers out and prisoners in. What Christ expects of us is not the building of earthworks or digging of foxholes. He wants us on the attack. Smashing Satan's defenses, destroying his weapons, setting his captives free.

That's offensive warfare. That's the Joshua style. It's my style, too. I hope it's yours.

We will not "hold what we've got" unless we're constantly fighting to take more of Satan's territory. There's no such thing as neutral ground; we're either advancing or retreating. Our enemy is constantly working against us and plotting our destruction. The Bible says we "wrestle not against flesh and blood" (Eph. 6:12; KJV) and we need to remember that. I was on the wrestling team in high school and college and I can tell you, you never let up in a match. If you try to back off and rest, the referee will penalize you for "stalling." If you don't scramble furiously when tangled up with your opponent, he will take advantage of the one second when you relax and he'll slam you on your back. You never let up in a match. You cannot win a wrestling match by fighting defensively.

And by the way, let's be clear on who it is that we're fighting. Satan is our enemy, and he alone. It's easy to get incensed at those who oppose us. It's very tempting to resent the liberal newscaster, the ACLU lawyer, the crooked politician who's trying to steal your money and your freedom. It's natural to be offended by the militant homosexual or the Satanist. But these people are flesh and blood. We're not fighting them. They're not the enemy. They are the captives of our enemy. Our job is to attack him, knock down his gates, and set them free.

At the National Home School Leadership Conference in Chicago in the fall of 2010, several of the invited speakers mentioned the possibility that persecution is coming to the Church in the near future, at least to those of us who are determined to train our children for Christ. They hadn't been comparing notes; it seemed to be a theme that just kept coming up. The conference hosts called our attention to it. They thought the Lord seemed to be trying to get a message across. There was a lot of talk about how we need to prepare for another wave of Satan's attacks.

Well, I was homeschooling in the 1980s, so I remember persecution and I definitely didn't like it. Home education wasn't clearly legal in most states back then, and our friendly neighborhood truant officer threatened to bring charges against my wife and me that could result in the state taking our children away from us. There was a period of months during which we trained our kids to run and hide under their beds whenever the doorbell rang. In America.

Well, let's assume Satan is planning more attacks. What should we do? Stop homeschooling, stop witnessing, stop worshiping in public? Hey, I've got an idea. Why wait for Satan to start a new wave of persecution? *How about we get busy persecuting him!* A plague on this circle-the-wagons mentality! Let's attack. Let's pray, let's fast, let's witness, let's write letters to the editor, let's get out the vote for worthy candidates, let's help the needy, let's raise up a standard. Let's destroy some strongholds.

Let's take back the land.

That's the challenge I'm offering you. I'm not asking if you can be a warrior for Jesus. I already know you can. I'm asking if you *will*.

America is in sad shape, but don't despair. Read your Bible and you'll see that God has brought revival and reformation to wicked societies many times in the past, sometimes even suddenly. He would have spared Sodom for the presence of just ten righteous men. He revolutionized Nineveh in just a couple of days, having nothing better to work with than one reluctant preacher who was so rebellious that it took three days in a fish's gut to get him going in the right direction. God hasn't changed. He's just as powerful as He has always been, and He expects His people to triumph, not surrender.

If you haven't figured it out by now, I don't have a lot of patience with doomsaying, defeatism, and compromise. I'm not particularly brave, but I can't see any excuse for not hating what God hates as much as loving what He loves and fighting for what Jesus died for. We already know we'll ultimately win. We will lose some battles, but our commander has already won the war — on the Cross.

I like people who think in terms of victory. Here are some quotes from men I admire:

In war, there is no substitute for victory.[2] — General Douglas MacArthur

The enemy is in front of us and behind us. They're on both sides of us. They can't get away this time![3] — General "Chesty" Puller

One of my favorite quotes comes from an unnamed World War II fighter pilot who somehow got separated from his squadron in battle and found himself facing a horde of Japanese planes on the other side of the Pacific island over which they were fighting: "Somebody come and give me a hand!" he shouted into his radio mike. "I've got 38 of 'em cornered over here!"

Okay, I hope I've convinced you that we're in a war and that we have a responsibility to fight to win. Now let's talk about how we're going to win it. Later in the book, we'll deal more specifically with the individual battlefields.

With Satan holding ground in so many areas of our culture, none of us can be involved in every battle. We don't have to be; God can handle any battle without you or me. The key is to find out which battles He does want us in and jump in with a vengeance.

There are three battlefields upon which all of us must fight: the family, the church, and the government. Why these three? Because they are the three God-ordained institutions that determine the spiritual temperature of a society. They all affect the others, so influence on one is influence on all, to some degree. We all have a family. As Christians, we are all responsible for the health of God's Church. As Americans, we are part of the government. Yes, I said part of the government. In America, We the People share the authority. That's the Constitution. We elect representatives, but they are our servants, not we theirs. They forget that sometimes, and that's why they need us to be involved.

Beyond these three unavoidable responsibilities, there are several other battlefields where you may be needed. In this war for the soul of America, there is plenty for each of us to do. But wherever God calls you to fight, don't fight to delay defeat — fight to conquer.

You are the Joshua generation. Take back the land.

Endnotes

1. John Taylor Gatto, *Dumbing Us Down: The Hidden Curriculum of Compulsory Schooling* (Philadelphia, PA: New Society Publishers, 1992).

2. http://quotationsbook.com/quote/41062.

3. http://www.freerepublic.com/focus/news/2355654/posts.

Chapter 3

LEADERSHIP: THE KEY TO VICTORY

Okay, I've just spent two chapters challenging you to forget adolescence and just go ahead and take your turn at the adult life. Now I'm going to take it a big step further.

One of the most important issues we face in life is the question of whether to live as a leader or a follower. Most of my generation, trained in public schools, grew up waiting to be told what to do, never much questioning whether what we were being told to do was really worth doing or whether there was a better way to do it. We got good at following instructions (whether they made sense or not), but we didn't get good at thinking for ourselves. We certainly weren't trained to think critically, come to our own conclusions, and persuade others to believe as we did. In other words, we were trained to be followers rather than leaders.

But why should you want to be a leader? Leaders have more responsibility. They take the blame when things go wrong, even when they had no control over the circumstances that led to the outcome. Leaders get blamed not only for their own failures, but for the failures of their followers, too. When the chips are down, the leader is the one who gets shot at most because the enemy knows that if they disable him, his followers will be confused and panicked. It's not easy being a leader. Who wants the hassle?

Hopefully, you do. Or will. The reason we have lost so much of our freedom as citizens and as Christians is because believers have forgotten how to think for themselves. We don't go to Scripture for our worldview and apply what we find there to our daily lives. We tend to believe what we read in the newspaper and see on television rather than being tenacious seekers of truth.

Even worse, we often act as if there's no such thing as truth. Maybe you've had the common experience of witnessing to somebody who says, "Hey, that's okay for you, if that's what you believe. That's great. But what's true for you might not be true for me. Everybody has to find his own truth, right?" Sounds soooo open-minded, non-judgmental, inclusive, and tolerant. Tolerance has become the modern American mantra.

The problem is that there *is* absolute truth. Denying it doesn't change the fact that it is. If you don't believe in absolutes, just take a dive from a tenth-story balcony. It won't matter whether you believe in gravity or not, honey. You're going to be a grease spot on the pavement. Turns out nature isn't all that tolerant.

Neither is God. When He says "Thou shalt" or "Thou shalt not," it would be a good idea to pay attention. And when Jesus said "I am the way, the truth, and the life: no man cometh unto the father but by me" (John 14:6; KJV), it was either absolutely true or absolutely false. On our response to that very absolute statement hangs our eternal destiny.

Hopefully, you believe in absolute truth. If you do, then you see that truth is important. If Jesus was speaking truth in John 14:6, then every other religion than Christianity is a lie. There is only one way to heaven, only one way to avoid hell. And that leads us to another important conclusion.

If we are persuaded of absolute truth, then we are obligated to persuade others also. If we know something that will help others, some truth the lack of which will condemn others to disaster, then we are responsible not only to inform them but to try to convince them of it. That's leadership.

A leader is one who knows what he believes and why he believes it. He lets that belief inform, prioritize, and discipline his life. Then he takes the next step. He tries to persuade others to adopt his beliefs for their own.

You know I'm not talking about forcing your beliefs on others. I'm talking about convincing them of the truth you believe, and that is sometimes much harder. But there's still another step to take.

A leader seeks to know what's right, do what's right, convince others of what is right, and *influence them to do what's right as well*. He doesn't do this by force; that's tyranny. He chooses what he believes is the right course of action whether anybody else believes it or not, and challenges others to join him. Many will — because they know that he hasn't chosen his course carelessly and they either want a leader to lead them or they're just convinced he's right.

Some people will follow a leader just because they're followers. These folks are either gullible, believing whatever they're told, or they're irresponsible and would rather follow the nearest leader than think for themselves. Others see the way the leader is going and become convinced that they should go along. Still others see the crowd moving after the leader and lose themselves in the mob because they're more comfortable doing that than forming their own opinions and values. In any case, rarely does a real leader lack for followers.

My challenge to you is to become a leader. We'll talk later in the chapter about how to prepare for leadership, but for now just start wrapping your mind around the idea. We live in a time of war: spiritual warfare and cultural warfare. You live in a country that was established on Christian principles and for a long time thrived on them. But for nearly a century, because of a lack of good leadership, we have been a nation in decline. Christians need to stand up and start changing the direction of our society instead of compromising and being drawn along with it. A few in my generation — just a few — stood up a quarter of a century ago and by God's grace won your freedom to be educated without government interference. Now it's your generation's turn to stand. The problems are huge, the challenges are Goliaths. But you'll find God's grace is still there.

In any war, the most important factor is leadership. Of course it's not only in war that leaders determine success or failure; any enterprise, whether an army, a family, or a business, rises and falls on the character and competence of its leaders. But we're talking warfare here so I'll stick with the military metaphors.

One of my favorite examples of leadership is General Thomas J. Jackson, alias Stonewall Jackson, of the Confederate army in the Civil War. In the summer of 1862 the Union army under General McClellan was advancing on Richmond, the capital of Virginia and the Confederacy. General Lee, the Confederate commander, knew he was outnumbered and that more Union troops were on the way from western Virginia under Generals Milroy, Banks, and Fremont. He ordered Stonewall Jackson, with a smaller army than any of the three Union generals, to do what he could to keep them busy so they couldn't join with McClellan and overwhelm Richmond.

Jackson was a devout Christian and a brilliant leader. He was also ferociously aggressive, driving himself and his men to the utmost of their endurance. His genius for warfare became a legend that summer, as he kept three enemy armies in confusion and their generals looking like fools. Stonewall would attack out of nowhere, wreak havoc on Fremont, then disappear into the woods. A few days later he would appear like a ghost and hit Milroy. He'd whip Milroy and slip away again, only to materialize in the rear of Banks and give him a beating. Then he'd be off again to plan his next attack.

None of the three Yankee armies could get anywhere near Richmond. Just when they thought they could regroup and head eastward, Stonewall would descend on them like a tornado. He kept them on the defensive — not with superior numbers but with superior leadership.

Think about this in the context of the Church. So much depends upon the faithfulness of the pastor. How many times have you heard of a church that was doing fine for a while, only to be torn apart when the pastor fell into immorality or made improper use of church funds? That's why Timothy tells us that a church leader carries extra responsibility and is liable to greater condemnation.

But returning to the military example, imagine a fine army under an incompetent general. His scouts report that the enemy has only half the men and weaponry that he himself has. Perfect time for an attack. Instead, the general has his men dig in and prepare for defense. Days go by and the opposition receives reinforcements. Now our General Chicken really is on the defensive. His superior army missed a chance to destroy the opposition because of poor leadership.

Adolph Hitler was an extraordinarily evil man but he understood leadership. He was a bad man with a devious brain and he took over Europe by developing unquestioning leaders.

Hitler rose no higher than the rank of corporal in the First World War, but in the desperate days of depression in Germany that followed, he joined the Nazi party and quickly rose to the top. Having taken over the Nazis, he showed them how to take over the country. Germany was desperate and he promised prosperity and a return to national greatness, so people believed in him. Hitler's radicalism frightened many people, but they overcame their misgivings because they knew they desperately needed leadership.

Hitler wanted revenge on the Allied powers that had defeated and humiliated Germany in World War I. But the Treaty of Versailles, which ended the war, prohibited Germany from rebuilding her army. She was limited to a small number of men and a very limited supply of weapons and material. What was Adolph to do?

For one thing, Hitler inspired and organized the civilian population. He mastered propaganda and gave the German people their national self-esteem back. He even created a "straw man" that the Germans could blame for their misfortune. By targeting the Jewish people, he is personally responsible for setting in motion the efforts to persecute, and ultimately murder, millions of innocent people by those who followed his leadership without question. He even organized young people in organizations such as Hitler Youth, complete with uniforms. There were marching bands and mass rallies and Hitler's raving, patriotic speeches that brought thousands of people to their feet screaming, "Heil Hitler!"

The civilians were being trained to accept leadership. At the same time, the army was being trained to supply it. Hitler hit on a brilliant scheme. Without increasing the size of his army — which could have triggered intervention from the Allies — he instead concentrated on training his men to *lead* the massive forces he planned to soon build. Every soldier was trained to do the job of the rank above him. Privates were taught to work as sergeants. Sergeants were trained as lieutenants, majors as colonels, colonels as generals. When at last he had grown so strong that England and France were hesitant to try reining him in, all he had to do was promote all his men to the rank above, then enlist hundreds of thousands of civilians to be trained as privates. After a few weeks of basic training for the new recruits, Hitler's army had gone from a skeleton crew to a formidable military force. Now too strong to be challenged, Hitler was soon invading and conquering the neighboring countries.

Do you see what happened here? Hitler concentrated on leadership, training even the privates in his little army to be ready to move up to sergeants when new followers were inducted. He knew that he would have no trouble recruiting followers because he was busily brainwashing the civilian population into automatons who thought of themselves as group members rather than individuals or family members. They were trained to be followers while an elite few, fiercely loyal to the government, were being trained to be leaders.

That's why the elite few didn't have to be the elite many. *It only takes a few strong leaders to move the masses in a chosen direction.* And that's why leaders had better be righteous people rather than wicked people.

It was great leaders that made an American nation out of 13 puny English colonies, and it is ungodly leaders that have brought America from being a truly God-fearing society to being a culture in apostasy. From about the 1930s to the present, Christians have largely fallen asleep to the spiritual warfare that has been dragging our country down. We have backed out of leadership and civic involvement, leaving the field largely to the pagans. Professing Christians are still by far the largest religious group in America, yet the minority rules. Only about 3 percent of Americans claim to be atheists, yet the courts have ruled that we can't pray or read the Bible in school. See? A minority is dictating to the majority because they have sympathetic people in positions of leadership, i.e., the Supreme Court.

Why has the majority of the national population stood by and allowed such things to happen? Because the majority have been trained to be followers, not leaders. And how was that done? In the public schools — schools controlled by the government and supported by the taxpayers so that only those wealthy enough to pay the taxes and tuition as well could afford to send their children to private schools. The vast majority of American kids are being taught in public schools. Sadly, about 90 percent of Christians send their children there as well.

They are taught evolutionary science to make them doubt the existence of God so that their moral values can be altered. They are divided into classes by age so that school separates them not only from their parents but from their siblings as well, to break down family loyalties. They are given plenty of mindless busy work to keep them from having time to think about their own questions about the world around them. They are shut off from the opportunity to make decisions for themselves, even when to go to the bathroom. These students are deliberately being conditioned to think the way their authorities want them to think. They are in training to be lifetime followers.

Now that you know all this, would you really be surprised to learn that the American public educational system came from Germany? That's right. Even before there was a modern nation of Germany, way back in the mid-1800s, American public school proponents were visiting the province of Prussia, later a part of Germany, to study their school system. Horace Mann, the first American state secretary of education (Massachusetts), was one of those early visitors. He brought back glowing accounts of the "success" of the Prussian schools in producing students who were compliant, passive, and susceptible to influence by their leaders. (See *The Underground History of American Education* by John Taylor Gatto.[1]) Good followers, people who wouldn't cause a lot of problems for the government. People who waited to be told what to do.

That's the soil from which American compulsory education sprang. If you're a homeschooler, that's what you avoided by being taught at home. Thank your parents.

Well then, where do American leaders come from? Good question. They come from a few elite private schools and colleges. They go through such "prep" schools as Groton, Exeter, and St. Paul's, then on to the Ivy League universities such as Harvard, Yale, and Princeton. Remember, these are the children of wealthy people, people often in leadership themselves in government or business. And if you think government and business aren't connected, you obviously aren't aware of how much the issue of money figures into political campaigns (do an Internet search for George Soros — it will be an eye opener).

In my own lifetime, the vast majority of American presidents and even candidates for president have been graduates of just a handful of elite universities. In fact, I was just reading an article reporting that every American president and almost every candidate for president of the last 20 years attended either Harvard or Yale. With the confirmation of Elena Kagan to the Supreme Court in 2010, every member of the present Supreme Court also attended Harvard or Yale.

So that's the way it worked from the late 1800s until the 1980s. The public schools trained the followers. A small minority of leaders were being trained in the private schools and universities. It was a cozy little system, at least for the wealthy elite. It kept the lower and middle classes in their place socially, and with each generation the populace grew less and less active in government. Big business was happy as fewer people had the initiative to start their own businesses, which might have competed with the older, established firms. Big labor (labor unions) benefited as well because fewer entrepreneurs meant more factory workers and more union members paying dues.

Then came the crack in the wall.

In the decade of the 1980s the world began to turn upside-down for the educational system. During that time (and with a few rare exceptions before that) parents across America began to get the idea that they could educate their own children. It was as if God were stirring up a little eddying breeze that began to gain strength and soon became a rushing wind. By 1990 the movement had grown to the point that most states had made some legal provision for home education. By 2000, everybody knew someone who was homeschooling, and homeschooled kids had established a record of excellence. Hundreds of colleges were recruiting them, they had won national academic contests and proven their competence in social affairs and business. Suddenly it was evident that there was a new source of leadership for America.

This is the movement that has produced you if you have been homeschooled. You were born into a country that started out avowedly Christian, enjoying all the blessings that result from honoring "the laws of nature and of nature's God," and had departed from that philosophy and much of that blessing. But your courageous parents bucked the social tide. Maybe your mom gave up a second income. Maybe your parents had to lobby the state legislature and fight for their rights in court, as our family did. Maybe they had to put up with criticism from relatives and church friends. One thing I can guarantee you: they haven't had an easy time. And now it's your turn to fight.

In one generation, God has raised up a new channel through which new American leadership is arising. It is the home education movement. As the Church of Jesus Christ began to awaken to the dangers of statism and secularism in the 1970s, we began to see our need and cry out to God for mercy, protection, and revival.

You are the answer to those prayers. Take it seriously. Like Esther in the Old Testament, God has put you where you are for such a time as this.

Hitler used the leadership principle in terrible and wicked ways. Today it's your job to use it in a God-honoring way. Professing evangelical Christians are really a majority in this country. But we've been acting like a minority — allowing ourselves to be pushed around, trying to hang on to what religious, economic, and personal freedom we have left. Wrong approach. Now we've seen that and started training our children to assert the truth of God in the public arena. Look out, Satan.

Leadership. Everything rises and falls on leadership. A strong leader, whether good or bad, will attract a following. That's why leaders carry such a huge responsibility — because they determine not only the direction of their own lives but the lives of others as well. For good or for evil, every leader's name is Legion.

Are you beginning to get the drift?

You are called to be a leader.

Yes, I mean you. You may or may not think you're leadership material. You may or may not want the responsibility. But God isn't giving you the option. He has set up His universe in such a way that everybody in some way has influence over the thinking and actions of others. That's leadership.

Look at Proverbs 12:26. In the NASB it says: "The righteous is a guide to his neighbor, but the way of the wicked leads them astray."

If you have been made righteous through the new birth, then you are a guide to those around you. After all, what is a guide but someone who shows you where to go, knowing the way by having been there before? That's leadership. Not driving people but leading them. Showing them the way.

Your leadership roles will change throughout your life. Someday you may be leading the nation. Right now you may be leading nobody but your little brother. Lead him well, because this job may just be a big part of your training for bigger leadership jobs later in life.

Different types of people have different roles in leadership. God has laid down ground rules in Scripture and we should observe them. He occasionally makes exceptions, but rules are still rules.

Normally, the older leads the younger. That just makes sense, as older people have more life experience to draw from in making decisions. But once in a while, God raises up a Josiah (see 2 Kings 22) who takes the throne very young and becomes a great king.

Normally, the male leads the female. Husbands lead wives. The Old Testament ordained priests, not priestesses. In the New Testament, men rather than women are called to be pastors. Today in some circles it's fashionable to call a pastor and his wife both "pastors" of the church, but that's not biblically proper. A woman can't be the "husband of one wife" (see 1 Tim. 3:2). Still, God has sometimes put women in leadership over men, as Deborah in Judges chapter 4. It's not His norm, but maybe He does it to shame men for not having done their job as leaders.

But young people do lead other young people. Women do lead other women. That's what Titus 2:3–5 is all about. So I repeat my thesis: Everybody is called to lead someone, somehow, and somewhere at some time.

You are called to be a leader.

A Word to the Women

Wait a minute, you say. I'm a girl. I don't want to be president of the United States, I want to get married and be a mom.

I say, bravo!

Girls are really getting a bum rap these days. The feminists insult them if they don't want to enter the workplace and compete with men for jobs traditionally held by men. The feminists take it as an insult if someone suggests that a woman can't do any job a man can do, and do it just as well . . . I say it's an insult to a woman to suggest that she doesn't have better things to do than compete with men.

This just in: It has been discovered that women and men are not the same thing!

There are a multitude of voices telling women they are not successful if they don't join the battle up the corporate work ladder. Success is defined by working overtime, networking with anyone and everyone to increase opportunity, and being tethered to a desk 24–7 with a smart phone and a priority of work first and next, with everything else struggling in a distant third place. But there is a biblical model of a working woman that has something to inspire any woman today.

Proverbs 31 presents the ideal of the Virtuous Woman. The woman who stands head and shoulders above others is described here in detail and yes, she is involved in the business world. Yes, she does earn money. Yet at the same time, both her children and her husband rise up and call her blessed. What is she doing right?

Well, look at how her business life is different from the average woman you know. The Virtuous Woman works, but she doesn't punch a time clock. She's an entrepreneur, a woman who works to build opportunity for her family. She keeps her priorities first, which is why her husband and kids don't feel neglected. She's self-employed and following the loving leadership of her husband and doesn't have a boss at work whose needs may sometimes conflict with her availability to family priorities. She takes pride in the quality of her workmanship. Her work locates her at home or in the public marketplace, but she doesn't experience the pressure to achieve at the cost of family nor deal with the immorality of co-workers. She is a successful operator of an enterprise (the field, the vineyard, her own home-based business), but business success is not the top priority of the Virtuous Woman.

This Superwoman puts her family first. She looks well to the needs of her household. She supports her husband. Not coincidentally, he is a successful man. It says he's known in the gates — a community leader — but it tells us nothing about his qualifications to be there. We read that his wife ministers to the community — she reaches out her hand to the poor, but all we are told about her husband is that he has an excellent wife and he knows it. There is tremendous power in the influence of a godly wife and mom.

Girls, I would never insult you by saying that you have to do what men do to be successful. You are able to do so much more than any man ever could. Lots of people could be president of the United States or a senator or a justice on the Supreme Court. Many could build a great business enterprise, but it takes a woman — a strong, godly woman — be a builder of lives.

You have the capacity to give life, care, and training to the boys who will one day be leaders "in the gates." You can do the same for the girls who will one day be Proverbs 31 women, whose love, wisdom, and self-sacrifice propel their husbands and children to true success in life. I'm not saying you couldn't be a national leader. I'm saying why settle for that when you could guide and inspire a whole family of national leaders. And future generations of leaders as well.

> I would give a woman not more rights, but more privileges. Instead of sending her to seek such freedom as notoriously prevails in banks and factories, I would design specially a house in which she can be free. —G.K. Chesterton[2]

Barbara Bush was the wife of a president, the mom of a president, and the mom of two governors. Rose Kennedy was the wife of a multimillionaire and mom of a president, a senator, and a U.S. attorney general (who probably would have been elected president had he not been assassinated). It's a safe bet those women didn't spend all their time working on an assembly line and playing bridge. Be a leader of women and produce leaders of men. We'd never have heard of Susannah Wesley had it not been for her sons John and Charles.

Don't take any of this as a put-down to moms who have to work. I say, God bless them. I was raised by a single mom who worked in an airplane factory operating a rivet gun for years. She finally damaged her hands so badly that she had to have surgery for carpal tunnel syndrome. Thousands of women find themselves in that situation and my hat is off to them. They have one of the world's hardest roles to play, balancing a job and a home. I have a workshop that I present for single homeschooling moms at conferences called "Son of a Single Mom: Hope for Families without Fathers." I have endless respect for these ladies, but still I believe there is a scriptural ideal and it needs to be aimed at, even though we sometimes miss.

But I'm Too Young to Be a Leader

No, you're not. Oh, you're exactly right that older people should be leaders. For instance, the pastor is supposed to be an elder. But there are a couple of things you need to keep in mind. First, there is somebody who looks up to you. If you're mature enough to read a book like this there are people, some younger than you and some not, who respect your opinion about something. You have an influence. Second, you need to be using your influence both to set an example for those who respect you and to gain experience for greater leadership later on. Being a big brother is good training for being a squad leader in Scouts. Being a squad leader is good experience for being a foreman at work later on. Use the influence you have now. Use it righteously and wisely. It will lead to more influence over more people as time goes on.

> Into the hands of every individual is given a marvelous power for good or evil — the silent, unconscious, unseen influence of his life. This is simply the constant radiation of what man really is, not what he pretends to be.[3] — William George Jordan

> Just by providing a good example as a parent, a friend, a neighbor makes it possible for other people to see better ways to do things. Leadership does not need to be a dramatic, fist in the air and trumpets blaring activity.[4] — Scott Berkun

Example is not the main thing in influencing others; it is the only thing.[5] — Albert Schweitzer

If your actions inspire others to dream more, learn more, do more, and become more, you are a leader.[6] — John Quincy Adams

But there's much more to the leadership picture. There are several ways you can contribute to good leadership even when you're not the leader yourself. Let's think outside the box here.

First of all, every leader needs *helpers*. It's hard to imagine how a person could even get in a position as leader without help. Even tyrants like Hitler have to have the help of somebody to gain authority over somebody else. Leaders also need people to help them do their jobs. All those people contribute to leadership.

Another way to provide leadership without being the leader is by *giving counsel* to leaders. This was Daniel's job in the Old Testament Book of Daniel. He was a main counselor to four, count 'em, four different kings. Kings came and went, but old Daniel survived through four different administrations. Today, every leader from the pastor to the president relies on advisors. Congressmen have pages and interns, judges have clerks. All leaders rely on their helpers for information, advice, and encouragement. Sometimes you can have more power by being in a position of influence than in a position of authority.

You can also play a huge part in leadership by helping to *select* leaders. There's a story, a parable if you will, in Judges 9:8–15 about how the trees of the field sought out a leader. The useful trees like the fig and the olive wouldn't take the job, so the poor trees finally had to settle for the bramble bush. That's a lesson for all of us: If good people don't accept the responsibility for leadership, we end up with bad leaders. That's another reason Christians should run for political office. But we should also seek out good candidates if we're not called to run ourselves.

> The led must not be compelled; they must be able to choose their own leader.[7] — Albert Einstein

I hope you see that you have a role in leadership. Somebody is looking up to you right now, and with every year that goes by you will have more influence over others. Use it. And use it in a godly way. The times are serious and the stakes are high.

And while you're still young and somewhat limited in the number of leadership roles you qualify for, remember that leadership is a big tent. There is room for those who lead, but there is always a need for those who recruit, train, counsel, assist, and serve leaders. Like Joshua, it may be in serving a great leader that you qualify for great leadership in the days ahead.

Such a time as this.

Endnotes

1. John Taylor Gatto, *The Underground History of American Education* (New York: Oxford Village Press, 2001).

2. (http://www.goodreads.com/quotes/show/97495.

3. http://www.readbookonline.net/readOnLine/22957.

4. http://www.lifehack.org/articles/lifehack/interview-with-scott-berkun.html.

5. http://quotationsbook.com/quote/12974.

6. http://thinkexist.com/quotation/if_your_actions_inspire_others_to_dream_more/339093.html.

7. http://www.searchquotes.com/quotation/The_led_must_not_be_compelled,_they_must_be_able_to_choose_their_own_leader/29152.

Chapter 4

PRINCIPLES OF REFORMATION

This book is about a new generation taking back America. I hope you understand that this country was built by Christians and that all its institutions — family, church, government, education — were led by people whose philosophy was Christian in nature. Though many different religions were present in early America, Christianity was dominant and it was understood that we were a Christian nation in law and culture. That philosophy was what guided us as a citizenry until very recently in our history. From the time of the Pilgrims and their Mayflower Compact, which was the predecessor of our Constitution, until at least the early 1960s when the Supreme Court officially broke our covenant with God by throwing Him out of the public schools, Christianity was acknowledged as our common culture.

That's why what we're talking about here is not a revolution. It is a counterrevolution — in that we are fighting to reestablish the culture that existed traditionally before the apostasy of the late 20th century. We're trying to return Christian principles to the public forum and to a place of prominence in the guiding philosophies of our institutions. It's a war of ideas, not swords. It's a war of love, not hate. And it must be won spiritually before it can be won ideologically.

Our war is similar to the one experienced by the Israelites who escaped slavery in Egypt. One generation departed from their homeland for the promise of greener pastures. Eventually, they found themselves enslaved. Another generation, through strong leadership and miraculous assistance from God, escaped the yoke of slavery. They left the foreign country and headed for their homeland through a wilderness of difficulties. They got part of their inheritance back, but much remained to be done when their children came of age to take over the battle. Across the Jordan there awaited a land flowing with milk and honey — a million blessings. But in their absence enemies had taken over their territory and built strongholds there. Looking across the river, the new generation saw their homeland, a land of abundance. They also saw enemy strongholds. It was their turn to fight.

Read through the following passage from Joshua chapter 1. Look for the parallels between the situation of Israel and the challenge you face as a young Christian warrior of 21st-century America.

> Now it came about after the death of Moses the servant of the LORD, that the LORD spoke to Joshua the son of Nun, Moses' servant, saying,
>
> Moses My servant is dead; now therefore arise, cross this Jordan, you and all this people, to the land which I am giving to them, to the sons of Israel.

Every place on which the sole of your foot treads, I have given it to you, just as I spoke to Moses.

From the wilderness and this Lebanon, even as far as the great river, the river Euphrates, all the land of the Hittites, and as far as the Great Sea toward the setting of the sun will be your territory.

No man will be able to stand before you all the days of your life. Just as I have been with Moses, I will be with you; I will not fail you or forsake you.

Be strong and courageous, for you shall give this people possession of the land which I swore to their fathers to give them.

Only be strong and very courageous; be careful to do according to all the law which Moses My servant commanded you; do not turn from it to the right or to the left, so that you may have success wherever you go.

This book of the law shall not depart from your mouth, but you shall meditate on it day and night, so that you may be careful to do according to all that is written in it; for then you will make your way prosperous, and then you will have success.

Have I not commanded you? Be strong and courageous! Do not tremble or be dismayed, for the LORD your God is with you wherever you go.

What was God's answer for the challenges ahead? A new generation of warriors following strong leadership. Joshua had been Moses' second-in-command and now the mantle was being passed on to him. He had been thoroughly trained and hardened in battle. He had watched Moses face challenge after challenge, watched him succeed and watched him fail. He had seen Moses fight the Egyptians

once but fight his own people for 40 years in the wilderness. He was
a seasoned warrior, having been a servant to the Moses generation.
Now it was his turn to lead and God intended for him to succeed.
It was time to cross the river. The Word of the Lord came to Joshua.
Notice what God said.

> Moses My servant is dead; now therefore arise, cross
> this Jordan, you and all this people, to the land which I am
> giving to them, to the sons of Israel (verse 2).

*It's your turn, Joshua. Your turn and that of your generation.
Cross the river. I intend to give you back the land I gave to your
forefathers.*

> Every place on which the sole of your foot treads, I have
> given it to you, just as I spoke to Moses.
> From the wilderness and this Lebanon, even as far as
> the great river, the river Euphrates, all the land of the Hit-
> tites, and as far as the Great Sea toward the setting of the
> sun will be your territory.
> No man will be able to stand before you all the days of
> your life. Just as I have been with Moses, I will be with you;
> I will not fail you or forsake you (verses 3–5).

*I have marked out your boundaries. With Me helping you, no en-
emy can stand against you. I will never fail you, I will never desert you.
I have already given you the land — every place on which the sole of
your foot treads — but you must cross the river and walk on it.*

> Be strong and courageous, for you shall give this people
> possession of the land which I swore to their fathers to give
> them (verse 6).

Be strong. That means prepare yourself. You have been trained in battle; keep training to maintain the strength you have acquired. Always be thinking of the battles ahead so that you stay ready.

Be courageous. I'm telling you in advance that you will win this war. You face a ferocious enemy who will not welcome you back to the land of your inheritance. He will strike you again and again so you must strike him and strike hard to keep him on the defensive. You must expect casualties: you will be wounded. But take courage from my promise of victory and share it with those who follow you.

> Only be strong and very courageous; be careful to do according to all the law which Moses My servant commanded you; do not turn from it to the right or to the left, so that you may have success wherever you go.
>
> This book of the law shall not depart from your mouth, but you shall meditate on it day and night, so that you may be careful to do according to all that is written in it; for then you will make your way prosperous, and then you will have success (verses 7–8).

I've told you to be strong and be courageous. Now I am telling you how. Be careful to do according to My law. Don't turn from it to the right or to the left. That's the key to your success. And by being careful to do according to it, I mean concentrate on it. Don't just check in once in a while looking for a proof text to back up your own opinion. I mean have it on your mind so you have it in your mouth. Think about it so much that it automatically comes out in all your councils of war. Meditate on My law day and night; that's the key to acting accordingly. Again I say, that is your key to victory.

> Have I not commanded you? Be strong and courageous! Do not tremble or be dismayed, for the LORD your God is with you wherever you go (verse 9).

Remember, I have issued the order. This is My war, not yours. Draw your strength and courage from that fact. The strongholds are mighty, the challenges are great. But never be intimidated by them, because I am with you always and I am the Lord.

I'll reiterate that I am NOT saying that this passage applies directly to the United States today. It was said in the context of the Israelite conquest of Canaan and that's how it was intended. What I am saying is that you are in a similar situation and that God's principles are unchanging. God still expects us to fight His enemies. He still promises to be with us in all our difficulties. He still promises that we will be victorious — not always in the temporal sense, but in the sense of spiritual victory regardless of worldly outcome. Remember, the Apostle Paul won his battles by taking the gospel even to Caesar's household. He was beheaded when God was through with him, not before. That's real victory.

So let's be committed to this war. It's a war for the soul of America. We're truly a city on a hill to which the rest of the world can look for a testimony of the blessings that come to a nation founded upon the principles of God's Word. More than that, America is the great launching pad for the gospel. More missionaries and more support for missions have gone forth from this country than any other nation. So when we fight for America we fight for all people everywhere.

Joshua was told that if he was to make his way prosperous and have success, he must meditate on God's Word. If we intend to win our war, we must look to that Word also for the principles of our strategy. Let's take a look at some of those principles and see how they apply to us and our mission.

1. It's a spiritual battle above all.

Revelation 12:10–11 gives us the requirements to defeat Satan:

Then I heard a loud voice in heaven, saying, "Now the salvation, and the power, and the kingdom of our God and the authority of His Christ have come, for the accuser of our brethren has been thrown down, he who accuses them before our God day and night. And they overcame him because of the blood of the Lamb and because of the word of their testimony, and they did not love their life even when faced with death."

The blood of the Lamb, the word of their testimony, and the willingness to sacrifice their lives. Let's look at each of these individually.

The blood of the Lamb comes first. If we are not redeemed by that blood, we still belong to the enemy. We are dead in trespasses and sins and have no life or power. But on the Cross, Jesus defeated Satan and paid for our salvation, nailing the certificate of debt (our sins) to the Cross. If we are born again as children of God, Satan has no power over us and no defense against us. The blood of the Lamb has sealed his fate. He's toast and he knows it.

We must proclaim that fact by the word of our testimony. We can't be silent. God has made the sacrifice and done the work. He has not sent angels, but men and women to tell the world about it. First and always that means preach the gospel to every creature. The word of our testimony is that Jesus is Lord. All power is given to him by the Father (Matt. 28:18) and that is the key to the Great Commission. By the word of our testimony we are to take that truth all around the world and make disciples of all nations, teaching them everything He has commanded. That includes speaking His truth into every area of culture.

They did not love their life, even when faced with death. Of course it's obvious that this means we must be willing to die for the

Lord. But it also means we must be willing to live for Him. Notice it says "even" when faced with death. Even? That means that we must be willing even to die, the ultimate sacrifice. But what lesser sacrifices precede the "even"? The Apostle Paul said, "I die daily," in 1 Corinthians 15:31. In the previous verse, he says that he is in danger every hour. In the following verse, he recalls having "fought with wild beasts" in Ephesus. He seems to be saying that though he has not yet given up his physical life to the cause of Christ, he daily lays down his life in the sense of doing and enduring whatever God may require in His service.

Dying daily means sacrificing my own rights, comfort, reputation, pleasures, relationships, plans, dreams, and freedom. It means I am a slave of Christ. I am willing to give it up for Him, every day. It means I don't have the right to choose my own friends. I don't have the right to choose my own music. I don't have the right to spend my time as I want or work where I choose or eat the foods that I like (ouch). Jesus may allow me some of those things as privileges and I'm thankful that He often does. But He is the boss and I have to stand ready to give up anything He calls for. To die to self.

Those are the three keys to winning our battles spiritually. That means prayer, prayer, and more prayer. We must dedicate ourselves to praying without ceasing if we want God's power in battle.

2. It's a long-term commitment.

First, let's dispense with the "last days" argument. No doubt you've heard somebody say that it's too late to save America because we're living in the last days and things are going to get worse and worse. I say that's the sorriest kind of a cop-out. God has never offered His people the option of quitting. Our job is to do our duty at all times and in all circumstances.

The passage people usually think of when they talk this way is 2 Timothy 3:1 and several verses following. Verses 1 and 2 say this:

> But realize this, that in the last days difficult times will come. For men will be lovers of self, lovers of money, boastful, arrogant, revilers, disobedient to parents, ungrateful, unholy. . . .

The Greek word for "last days" is *eschatos*. It means the last in succession. Contextually, it's a good translation. Paul is writing to Timothy about the last days. But notice that in the following verses he uses the present tense in talking about the sorry characters that men will be in the last days. In verse 5 he warns Timothy to avoid such men:

> Holding to a form of godliness, although they have denied its power; avoid such men as these.

Obviously, those men were already around, or at least would be during Timothy's lifetime. Verse 6 shows that he is talking about the present rather than the future:

> For among them are those who enter into households and captivate weak women weighed down with sins, led on by various impulses. . . .

"Among them *are*" — not *were*. Verse 8 adds that these men "oppose" not "opposed" the truth. Present tense. The last days had already started in Timothy's day.

Want more? Look at Hebrews, first chapter. The first verse talks about how God spoke to men in former times. Verse 2 says that at the time of that writing, God had spoken through Jesus. Look how the author refers to his present time:

God, after He spoke long ago to the fathers in the prophets in many portions and in many ways, in these last days has spoken to us in His Son, whom He appointed heir of all things, through whom also He made the world (Heb. 1:1–2).

Note he says in "these" last days. The last days had started in the first century. And yes, "last days" here is again translated from *eschatos*. Same Greek word as in 2 Timothy 3. Now one more reference in Acts 2:

But Peter, taking his stand with the eleven, raised his voice and declared to them: "Men of Judea and all you who live in Jerusalem, let this be known to you and give heed to my words. For these men are not drunk, as you suppose, for it is only the third hour of the day; but this is what was spoken of through the prophet Joel: 'AND IT SHALL BE IN THE LAST DAYS,' God says, 'THAT I WILL POUR FORTH OF MY SPIRIT ON ALL MANKIND; AND YOUR SONS AND YOUR DAUGHTERS SHALL PROPHESY, AND YOUR YOUNG MEN SHALL SEE VISIONS, AND YOUR OLD MEN SHALL DREAM DREAMS' " (Acts 2:14–17).

See the phrase "last days" in verse 16? *Eschatos* again. The last days had started at the beginning of the church age.

So yes, we are living in the last days. So was the Apostle Paul. Every generation since the Resurrection has thought it was the last generation. I hope we're right this time. But whether Jesus comes today or a thousand years from now, our responsibility is unchanged. We are to do His business until He comes. That's the meaning of the parable in Luke 19: A nobleman went on a journey and entrusted money to his servants to invest while he was away. He told them,

"Occupy until I come." The Greek word for occupy means "do business." The master was telling his servants to carry on his business until his return.

Jesus is saying the same thing to us. *Do My business until I come. Preach the gospel. Feed the poor. Care for the sick. Protect the rights of the afflicted.* There's no provision in there for retirement. Even if we're living in the last days of the last days, we can't close up shop. So if you've been one of those who wring their hands and moan about how things are just going to get worse and worse and we can't do anything about it — stop sniveling and get back to work.

We didn't get into this mess in one year and we probably won't get out of it in one year. While that's possible with God (remember Nineveh), historically it hasn't usually happened that way. We need to think in terms of generations. A number of times in Scripture, God answered the prayers of His oppressed people but took a generation to do it. Look what happened in Judges 13:1–5:

> Now the sons of Israel again did evil in the sight of the LORD, so that the LORD gave them into the hands of the Philistines forty years.
>
> There was a certain man of Zorah, of the family of the Danites, whose name was Manoah; and his wife was barren and had borne no children. Then the angel of the LORD appeared to the woman and said to her, "Behold now, you are barren and have borne no children, but you shall conceive and give birth to a son. Now therefore, be careful not to drink wine or strong drink, nor eat any unclean thing. For behold, you shall conceive and give birth to a son, and no razor shall come upon his head, for the boy shall be a Nazirite to God from the womb; and he shall begin to deliver Israel from the hands of the Philistines."

One generation sinned and brought God's judgment on their nation. No doubt they were praying for deliverance and hoped it would come quickly like a sudden rainstorm. But God gave them time to learn their lesson. He brought the answer to prayer in the next generation. Of course that's not the only instance of this happening. The birth of Jesus, the great Deliverer, was prophesied for thousands of years before He appeared. And in Judges chapter 6 we read of a similar occurrence as Israel sinned and was delivered into the hand of Midian. God raised up a young man, Gideon, to deliver the nation. Maybe you're the Gideon for America.

Revivals can be long-term things. The revival that birthed America was called the Great Awakening and lasted from around 1700 to the War of Independence. That's about 75 years. We in the microwave generation don't like waiting, but sometimes it takes time to get God's work done. It takes time to change cultural attitudes and longer to translate those attitudes into action. So buckle down for the long haul and don't be discouraged if you don't see what you're hoping for right away. You'll reap in due time if you keep on keeping on.

> For the one who sows to his own flesh will from the flesh reap corruption, but the one who sows to the Spirit will from the Spirit reap eternal life. Let us not lose heart in doing good, for in due time we will reap if we do not grow weary. So then, while we have opportunity, let us do good to all people, and especially to those who are of the household of the faith (Gal. 6:8–10).

I believe the homeschooling movement is the first wave in a national revival. It is now about 30 years old, about one generation. It's predicted to be the next "mega-movement" to sweep across the country and I believe it. What an exciting time in history! The Moses generation has escaped from bondage and the Joshua generation is at the river. Go get 'em!

3. Incrementalism

> The Lord your God will clear away these nations before you little by little; you will not be able to put an end to them quickly, for the wild beasts would grow too numerous for you (Deut. 7:22).

There's an interesting principle here. The context is Israel's pending invasion of Canaan. God promises to deliver the land into Israel's possession but says He won't do it quickly. Why not? Because the wild beasts would grow too numerous. God knows better than the Israelites. No doubt they would have suggested sending a plague among the Canaanites so they could be conquered without so much stress. But if God had done that, the cleared land would have grown back up in brush and weeds before Israel could move in and manage things. The wild predators such as wolves, which had been kept under control by the presence of millions of humans, could have multiplied to impossible numbers. Israel might have moved into the new country to find ruined vineyards and have their sheep all eaten by wolves. So God's plan was to clear out the enemy gradually.

It will be that way for us, too, I expect. If today God gave us control of government, the media, etc., there aren't enough of us trained to take care of the responsibility. It wouldn't be good to suddenly have control of Congress and not understand the process of how a bill becomes law or the tenets of parliamentary procedure. The wise way to approach the strongholds in society is for a young generation of committed Christians to infiltrate the strongholds, learn the ropes, and gradually rise to leadership. We may not like the condition of our national institutions at present, but at least they're being held together by the management.

We need to be training more leaders at the lower levels so that as opportunities arise we have people trained and ready to fill them. That's why we need to be running good people for office at the local and state level; that's where national leaders get their start. Teachers become administrators, rookie doctors grow into AMA leaders.

Baby steps are a good start. Slow progress is not *no* progress. As Ben Franklin said, "By little and little the mouse ate into the cable" (*Poor Richard's Almanac*). He meant one of those huge hemp ropes, several inches thick, that held ships to their dock moorings. Even a tiny mouse could loose a great ship if it was determined to succeed in little bites. Maybe you can't do much today, but do what you can. It will add up. And God will honor it.

4. Leadership

I've talked about this a lot already, but it needs to be seen in the context of revival and reformation. It's one of the key elements.

In the Book of Jonah, God sent one preacher to revive a city. In 2 Kings 22 and 23, God sent revival to the nation of Judah through young King Josiah. During the Great Awakening, the Lord gave such leaders as John and Charles Wesley and George Whitefield in England and Jonathan Edwards and the Tennents in America. There were other famous preachers of the day, as well, though we don't hear as much about them. But together they exerted enough influence on the culture of their day that it led to the formation of the new nation, the United States of America.

Whitefield preached to crowds of many thousands outdoors, which was in itself a pretty unusual thing. He crossed the Atlantic several times to preach in the colonies and traveled from Georgia all the way up to Maine. Whitefield preached to so many crowds that over 80 percent of all the people of the colonies heard him preach in person. That would be pretty amazing even today, with the means of transportation we have now. In those times when travel was by foot, wagon, and horseback, it seems nothing less than miraculous. But it was dedicated leaders like Whitefield that gave the revival its direction.

Today, God has raised up several people who are obviously anointed for a special work. Among these, I personally would include Bill Gothard of the Institute in Basic Life Principles (he has been used to bless me more than any other speaker I've heard), David Barton of Wallbuilders (God has been using him to restore our Christian heritage as a nation), and Ray Comfort, the evangelist from New Zealand whom God brought to America to tell us why we need to discard our easy-believism evangelistic methods and return to the biblical method of preaching the law to bring sinners to Christ. No doubt there are many others whom God is using in a powerful way. I hope some of the young people who read this book will join them on God's list of mighty men of valor in time.

Each of the leaders I mentioned has a ministry that is vastly different from the others. It seems that God raises up different servants for different needs and with different strengths. And sometimes a leader sees his ministry change in direction from time to time, like Elijah, who at one time was rebuking an evil king, at another time exposing the false prophets on Mount Carmel, and at another time ministering to a poor widow. As you and your parents pray about your present and future ministry, keep in mind that what you start doing in the Lord's work may not be where you spend the rest of your life. The important thing is to be willing to work anywhere He may put you.

You're young now and that means that you don't have as many options for leadership as you will later. So you need to do two things: lead where you can and support older leaders however you can. You don't even have to be a leader to provide leadership. You can do it by recruiting, serving, helping, and praying for leaders.

I'm excited to watch as the Lord does His work across America. In the next few years I expect to see Him raise up leaders in areas of our culture that have long been neglected for ministry. When that happens, we will see helpers flock to serve these leaders and big holes will be blown in Satan's strongholds in those areas. That's good. Satan needs to be on the receiving end of the persecution for a change.

One of the most important jobs of leadership in a revival is to train replacement leaders to carry on the work. There is no success without a successor, and wise leaders know this. Those of us who serve on the leadership boards of homeschooling organizations are mostly older people who remember the 1980s and how we had to struggle for the right to educate our children as we see fit. Many of us are determined to stay in those positions even after our own children are all grown up. We want to share our experience with younger people and train leadership who will move forward with the 1980s in mind. We don't want to leave our work in the hands of people who don't know about the struggle we had back then and might let their guard down, not understanding what a fragile thing freedom is.

The exciting thing is that new leaders are often more effective than the ones they replaced. Jesus told His disciples that they would do greater works than He had done Himself. Elijah trained Elisha and Elisha did twice as many miracles as his trainer. I believe that you in the Joshua generation will do far more for God than we in the Moses generation. There will be more of you fighting the good fight, and you have grown up without a lot of the spiritual and intellectual baggage that your parents and I carry.

5. *Opposition*

When Whitefield, Wesley, and their comrades started field preaching, they were quickly branded as heretics by the official church. That was partly because it was unorthodox, since the tradition was for preaching to stay inside the walls of the church building. It was also because thousands of people responded to these field preachers and the old masters were jealous. Later, when Whitefield was preaching in the colonies, he arrived in Boston city where an Establishment minister met him with the words, "I am sorry to see you here." Whitefield replied, "So is the devil."[1]

Not all the opposition came from the clergy. Many times the revival preachers — and their followers, too — were attacked by ruffians who didn't appreciate their efforts. Whitefield was once hit in the mouth by a flying rock as he preached. He kept right on preaching.

Remember this when you try to accomplish some goal for God. Not everybody will appreciate you, maybe not even those you're trying to help. But the duty is yours, the results are God's. Expect opposition. The only believers who don't get it are those the enemy feels he can afford to let alone. They're not a threat to him.

The next time you try to do something for God and run into opposition, read back through the first 12 chapters of Exodus. You'll find that Moses met opposition in trying to free his people from slavery. Pharaoh wouldn't listen, even though God had given Moses supernatural power to work miracles. And he was hardened even when God brought ten different plagues on his country. That's one hardheaded dude. In fact, Pharaoh was so hostile that he made the work of the enslaved Israelites even harder when Moses asked for their freedom. Finally, after the death of his firstborn son and all the other firstborns of Egypt, he submitted to Moses' demand. But later he changed his mind again and sent the army to bring Israel back. Bad move.

So don't be discouraged when you run into difficulties and detractors. Check yourself to make sure this isn't a reproof from God for wrong direction, wrong timing, or wrong methods, but if it's none of those things, then you can fight your way forward with confidence. You're doing something right if the enemy can't afford to let you go on unmolested.

6. A strong offense

I'm not sure who said it but one of my favorite quotes is, "The best defense is a good offense." That's true in football, it's true in boxing, and it's true in spiritual warfare. It was pointed out to me recently that when Christians fight defensively, they always lose. An example of this is in politics. When we spend all our time trying to keep bad bills from being passed into law, we're not writing and proposing good bills. Some Christian lawmakers are beginning to see this, so they're writing tons of new bills of their own. Now the opposition is having to spend time and resources on defending against our bills, so they have less to spend on introducing bad legislation. I love it. Let's take the fight to them.

Another example is the fight in the courts. In the early 1960s the Supreme Court made three landmark decisions that took prayer and Bible reading out of schools. For the next 40 years Christian legal groups fought on the defensive as atheist Madeline Murray O'Hare and the ACLU attacked everything from manger scenes on public property to crosses in cemeteries. We defended against lawsuit after lawsuit and lost pretty consistently. Then groups like American Center for Law and Justice and the Alliance Defense Fund began to go on the offensive, filing suits of their own, and we started winning. ACLJ president Jay Sekulow has been before the

Supreme Court about ten times and he has won his case every time. God is honoring offensive warfare in His name.

Proverbs 21:22 says:

> A wise man scales the city of the mighty and brings down the stronghold in which they trust.

That's offensive warfare, scaling city walls. Remember what I said about the "gates" of hell?

7. Everybody has a place on the battle line

The Book of Nehemiah is a great story of cultural warfare. Jerusalem was defenseless, her walls having been broken down when Israel was conquered by her enemies as a judgment for apostasy. Years later, some of the Israelites who had been captured and deported to Babylon were permitted to return to Jerusalem and rebuild the walls. Ezra the scribe had gone before and, despite much opposition, had rebuilt the temple. But when some of the exiles who had returned to Jerusalem went back to Babylon, they brought a report to Nehemiah, trusted Jewish assistant to the king, that the city walls still lay in ruins, leaving the city open to attack from her enemies.

When Nehemiah heard this, he was grieved. It was great that traditional worship of Jehovah had been restored, but any attacking force could run roughshod over the city and destroy it all again if the walls weren't repaired. So he asked the king for permission and material to go back and rebuild the walls. Again there was opposition, but finally he was successful. The walls stood tall and strong again.

There are important parallels between Jerusalem then and America now. We, too, have drifted away from our godly founding principles and we, too, are reaping consequences. Look around you at the assortment of moral, social, and even economic problems we're facing as a nation. We're vulnerable.

But Christians are beginning to understand how serious our situation is and to respond. I believe there is more prayer going up for America than there has been for a long, long time. Just as God used Ezra to restore worship in Jerusalem, He seems to be stirring the dry bones for us, too. I'll say again, I think the home education movement is the beginning of revival.

Behind Ezra, the religious leader, came Nehemiah, the civic leader. He had obtained the king's support in rebuilding the walls and he knew how to organize the residents of Jerusalem to get the job done. He got everybody involved so that the work went quickly. And even though their enemies were so venomous that they sometimes had to work with a sword in one hand, everybody had their place on the wall and they worked.

If we want revival and reformation in America, we need Ezras and Nehemiahs in leadership. We need to give the enemy a double whammy of spiritual and civic activism. We need to be prayer warriors — note that Ezra restored spiritual life first — and we need to do the work at the temporal level, too. Every Nehemiah needs Ezras supporting him in prayer. Every Ezra needs Nehemiahs to pray specifically for.

In Nehemiah chapter 3, we see that different people worked on different sections of the wall. Like them, we all want to see the whole wall rebuilt for America. But we can't all work everywhere. Just as Eliashib built the sheep gate and Ezer repaired the wall by the armory, each of us must find his own place of service. Nobody can do everything, but everybody must do something.

We also must be ready to jump in and help each other when one of us is especially threatened. Look what Nehemiah did when the work was threatened by enemies from without:

As for the builders, each wore his sword girded at his side as he built, while the trumpeter stood near me. I said to the nobles, the officials and the rest of the people, "The work is great and extensive, and we are separated on the wall far from one another. At whatever place you hear the sound of the trumpet, rally to us there. Our God will fight for us" (Neh. 4:18–20).

If the enemy attacked from the north, the workers there would sound the trumpet and some of the men would leave the other walls and rally to reinforce them. Same thing if a different wall was attacked. And so it is today in our warfare. Somebody whose main passion is politics keeps track of developments in Congress and when a bill is introduced that would threaten us, he sounds the trumpet (usually by e-mail) and a bunch of us temporarily drop our work in charity or the arts or evangelism and run to write our congressman about this bill. When the threat subsides, we get back to our own place on the wall.

Another interesting point to see here is that they prepared to fight by families.

When the Jews who lived near them came and told us ten times, "They will come up against us from every place where you may turn," then I stationed men in the lowest parts of the space behind the wall, the exposed places, and I stationed the people in families with their swords, spears and bows. When I saw their fear, I rose and spoke to the nobles, the officials and the rest of the people: "Do not be afraid of them; remember the Lord who is great and awesome, and fight for your brothers, your sons, your daughters, your wives and your houses."

When our enemies heard that it was known to us, and
that God had frustrated their plan, then all of us returned
to the wall, each one to his work (Neh. 4:12–15).

If we want to be victorious in battle, we had better learn to respect the family as a fighting unit. I'm all for the many great youth
organizations like TeenPact, Worldview Academy, and others who
exist to train young people for cultural warfare. Praise God for
them. But I'm not the only one who has observed that young people
who don't have their parents involved in their ministry efforts have
a harder time staying focused and sticking with it. The CEO of
TeenPact told me personally that the young people who go through
their training and come back later as TeenPact leaders are almost
always those whose parents are involved with them. So as you seek
the battles that God wants you fighting in, seek your parents' counsel and look for ways to work together with them. Fight as a family.

These are some principles to keep in mind as you prepare for
cultural warfare. The battle we face is not an easy one and probably
won't be a quick one. But how would you rather spend your life
than fighting for Christian causes? While some of your friends are
wasting their lives chasing every new pleasure that comes along, you
can be investing yourself in things that last forever.

Endnotes

1. http://www.e-steeple.com/browse-by-topic/W/Warfare,+spiritual.html.

Chapter 5

THE CHALLENGE

If American culture and our freedom are to survive much longer, your generation must get involved in governing our country. I say this without apology and without hesitation. It's no exaggeration. You guys must save America from tyrannical people in government or your children will not grow up free.

If it sounds like I'm trying to scare you, I am. It's scary to think how much freedom we've lost just in my lifetime, which in the scope of America's past is a comparatively short time. I was a kid in elementary school when the three Supreme Court rulings were handed down that ended our freedom to pray and read the Bible in the public school classroom. At that time (early 1960s), taxes for the average American were a fraction of what they are now. There was no Environmental Protection Agency, which has now acquired power it was never intended to have and stands as a major impediment to the right that property owners have to use their property as they see fit — including the filling in of swampy areas to control mosquito reproduction (in the name of preserving "wetlands").

Thus, in just a half century we have lost vast amounts of our freedom of religion, economic freedom, and property rights. But this is just the tip of the iceberg. The things I've mentioned represent a tsunami of government encroachment on your freedom as Americans. If you don't stand up in your generation and get involved, the next generation will grow up in an America that would be unrecognizable to our founders.

I'm giving government a lot of air time in this book because you need to understand how it works and give it your careful attention as a Christian citizen. But although I'm giving it individualized treatment, don't think that it doesn't overlap with the other battlefields as well. In fact, government has grown (meaning individual freedom has shrunk) so much since our founding that it now has its tentacles into virtually every facet of our lives. If we reclaim government by the people, we will radically expand freedom in our families, churches, business, education, and on and on.

The Church's Failure

Why has this happened? There are all kinds of political and social factors involved, but I believe that underlying all the decline is this simple fact: the Church in America has fallen down on the job. That's it in a nutshell.

We can justly point fingers at the Congress, the courts, the presidency, and so on, but we ultimately have ourselves to blame for what's happened to our country. God has allowed judgment to fall on America because the Church has failed in her job of being salt and light.

We have failed to get God's Word out into the public forum. Hardly anybody even knows what it says anymore, let alone believes and obeys it. Contrast that with first-century believers who were accused by even their enemies of having "filled Jerusalem with [their] doctrine" (Acts 5:28; NKJV).

We have failed to provide a convicting example of godly behavior to stand as a reproof to the lives of others around us. Divorce, for instance, is just about as common in the Church as outside of it. Teen rebellion and irresponsibility are just about the same as in the unchurched community. We're supposed to be the light of the world. How much light can we be shedding when the people all around us see no difference between us and the moral darkness in their own lives?

God forgive us, we have even failed to evangelize. We're gathering in our little enclaves each Sunday, enjoying the worship and fellowship, and few of us ever even take evangelism seriously enough to drop the occasional gospel tract.

All these failures are real and serious. But for the purposes of this chapter, we need to concentrate on our failure as a church to do our part in the governing of our country.

Why the Church Should Be Involved in Government

I'm sure you've heard some Christians say that politics is unspiritual, a dirty business that believers shouldn't soil their hands with. We need to concentrate on spreading the gospel and doing the works of Jesus, they say. Jesus didn't advocate political activism. In fact, He made a point of saying that His kingdom is not of this world.

All quite true. But Jesus didn't mind addressing the issue of misused authority, and neither did His followers. When He heard that His life had been threatened by King Herod, He referred to the king as "that fox" (Luke 13:32) and made it plain that the wicked ruler's pronouncements would in no way alter His plans for ministry. As for the religious leaders, He was known to call them a brood of vipers (Matt. 12:34).

John the Baptist used the same strong words for corrupt leaders (Matt. 3:7), and the Apostles made it clear that they had the responsibility to disobey human authority when it opposed God's authority (Acts 4:18–19). And the Apostle Paul was many times punished for civil disobedience and was known to write epistles from prison.

But as American Christians, there is an entirely different reason that we can, and in fact should be, involved in political issues. We have a dual citizenship. We are citizens of earth, the United States in particular, as well as citizens of heaven. We have obligations to both countries.

In some countries today, Christians have no freedom to be involved in the political process. In America it is the opposite. Not only can we have an influence on government, we are obligated to do so. Because in America, we citizens *are* the government. The American republic is a government of the people, by the people. Our leaders are not our bosses, rather we are theirs. They are our *representatives*. They represent us; they don't rule us. We have the power to hire and fire them with every successive elective cycle.

The Constitution of the United States is our basic founding document. It is the basis of our entire government. The founders who wrote it envisioned a nation in which the people were ruled by no man, no king, but were self-governing. That's why the Preamble (introduction) to the Constitution says:

> We the people of the United States, in order to form
> a more perfect union, establish justice, insure domestic
> tranquility, provide for the common defense, promote the

general welfare, and secure the blessings of liberty to c
selves and our posterity, do ordain and establish this Constitution for the United States of America.

In this one long sentence is set forth the great principle of
American freedom. The Declaration of Independence, written
over a decade earlier, had declared that "all men are created equal,
and that they are endowed by their Creator with certain unalien-
able rights," and now the new nation, formerly 13 English colonies
who had won their independence from Great Britain, was setting
up a new form of government that would ensure those rights. Note
that the first line of the Preamble says, "We the people," and if you
look at a picture of the original Constitution, you will find that
they wrote most of the phrase in capital letters. They meant, WE
THE PEOPLE are setting up this new nation. Then they went
on to set down the rules by which they would elect and send to
Congress the people they chose to *represent* them — not rule over
them.

Don't get me wrong, I firmly believe in the authority of government and law. God ordained it. But here's the difference between
the American republic and other forms of government: in America,
the PEOPLE are the authority. Their leaders are supposed to represent them, having been chosen by majority vote.

Look at it this way. In the old European monarchies, one man
was king. At his pleasure, every other citizen of the kingdom lived
and died. He had absolute authority. In America, every citizen is
king. We just have to share the authority. And since there are many
of us and we can't all go to Washington and vote on laws, we select
representatives to represent us. So America is a nation with over 300
million kings. And you're one of them. You just have to share the
job. This is not a silly play on words; it is a rock-solid fact. So accept

the fact that you are one of the kings of America and think about the words of the mother of another king, Solomon of Israel:

> What, my son? and what, the son of my womb? and what, the son of my vows?
>
> Give not thy strength unto women, nor thy ways to that which destroyeth kings.
>
> It is not for kings, O Lemuel, it is not for kings to drink wine; nor for princes strong drink:
>
> Lest they drink, and forget the law, and pervert the judgment of any of the afflicted.
>
> Give strong drink unto him that is ready to perish, and wine unto those that be of heavy hearts.
>
> Let him drink, and forget his poverty, and remember his misery no more.
>
> Open thy mouth for the dumb in the cause of all such as are appointed to destruction.
>
> Open thy mouth, judge righteously, and plead the cause of the poor and needy (Prov. 31:2–9; KJV).

What is the Queen Mother saying? She's saying, "Son, you're a king, and that's a lot of responsibility. So beware of temptations that will weaken you. Keep yourself strong and clearheaded so you can do your job with the wisdom it deserves. Be sure you use your authority for the advancement of righteousness."

As I said before, in America we share the authority but we are all kings and must take the responsibility seriously. What would you think of a judge who kept putting off making an important judgment? You'd say he wasn't a righteous judge. Justice, the rule of law, and the welfare of innocent people depend on his job performance. He ought to do the job or hang it up. Of course, you'd be right.

What then should we think of a Christian who has not only the right to vote, but the power to influence the votes of his family, friends, and acquaintances, and doesn't do anything about it? We should think he ought to do the job or hang it up. But we can't hang up our responsibilities as Americans — unless we renounce our citizenship.

Our responsibilities go far beyond the ballot box, but you see what I mean through this one example. In America, the people rule. You are just as responsible before God to do your share of governing as any king of Israel; you just have to share the authority with the rest of us.

And there's another thing to consider. Look what Romans 13 says about government leaders:

> For he is the minister of God to thee for good. But if thou do that which is evil, be afraid; for he beareth not the sword in vain: for he is the minister of God, a revenger to execute wrath upon him that doeth evil.
>
> Wherefore ye must needs be subject, not only for wrath, but also for conscience sake.
>
> For for this cause pay ye tribute also: for they are God's ministers, attending continually upon this very thing (Rom. 13:4–6; KJV).

What's that? Leaders are God's ministers? And some Christians say we shouldn't be involved in selecting God's ministers. Then who in the world should be doing it?

You'll hear people say that because politics is a dirty business, Christians shouldn't be involved. The correct answer to that is that politics is dirty because Christians aren't involved. Politics has been left to dirty people. If you've been cleansed by the blood of Christ, then the dirtier the arena, the more you're needed there.

William Booth, the founder of the Salvation Army, used to be criticized by his fashionable Christian friends for preaching on street corners in the slums to whatever prostitutes, addicts, and drunkards would listen. "What in the world are you doing, hanging around with such riffraff?" they wanted to know. He would reply, "I want a pulpit right on the edge of hell." And he went right on preaching.

He was right. He wasn't hanging out with those people because he intended to let them bring him down, but because he wanted to be used of God to bring them up. If that's your heart's cry as well, get involved in politics and let your light shine there. You'll have the same advantage in politics that Booth had in the slums: he didn't run out of sinners and neither will you.

Can the presence of believers make a difference in the civic arena? Scripture says it will:

> When it goes well with the righteous, the city rejoices, and when the wicked perish, there is joyful shouting.
>
> By the blessing of the upright a city is exalted, but by the mouth of the wicked it is torn down (Prov. 11:10–11).
>
> When the righteous increase, the people rejoice, but when a wicked man rules, people groan (Prov. 29:2).

Quite the contrary to the stay-out-of-politics position President James A. Garfield (who was also a minister of the gospel) said in 1877:

> Now more than ever before, the people are responsible for the character of their Congress. If that body be ignorant, reckless, and corrupt, it is because the people tolerate ignorance, recklessness, and corruption. If it be intelligent, brave, and pure, it is because the people demand these high qualities to represent them in the national legislature. . . . If

the next centennial does not find us a great nation . . . it will be because those who represent the enterprise, the culture, and the morality of the nation do not aid in controlling the political forces.[1]

Evangelist Charles Finney said in 1855:

> The Church must take right ground in regard to politics. . . . The time has come that Christians must vote for honest men, and take consistent ground in politics, or the Lord will curse them. They must be honest men themselves, and instead of voting for a man because he belongs to their party . . . they must find out whether he is honest and upright, and fit to be trusted. They must let the world see that the church will uphold no man in office, who is known to be a knave, or an adulterer, or a Sabbath-breaker, or a gambler, or a drunkard. . . . And if he will give his vote only for honest men, the country will be obliged to have upright rulers. All parties will be compelled to put up honest men as candidates.[2]

Even in Finney's day, some Christians were failing to exercise their responsibility to help select leadership, and he had little patience with them:

> Christians have been exceedingly guilty in this matter. But the time has come when they must act differently, or God will curse the nation, and withdraw his spirit. . . . God cannot sustain this free and blessed country, which we love and pray for, unless the church will take right ground. Politics are a part of religion in such a country as this, and Christians must do their duty to the country as a part of their duty to God. It seems sometimes as if the foundations

of the nation were becoming rotten, and Christians seem to act as if they thought God did not see what they do in politics. But I tell you, he does see it, and *he will bless or curse this nation, according to the course they take* (emphasis added).[3]

When Finney says that "politics are a part of religion in a country such as this," he didn't mean that politics can save anybody spiritually. He meant that in America, we Christians have a responsibility to do good through politics, just as we have to do good through evangelism or charity. In other countries, Christians may have no direct influence on the government. But here we do, and we must.

Garfield and Finney were active in politics in the mid-1800s, but long before that — even before and during our founding era — it was understood that as God has purposes for human government, His people should do all they can to influence it according to biblical principles. In fact, our founders recognized that, committed as they were to a republican form of government, it was much more the character of the people in office that determined God's blessing on a nation than the system of laws it had.

William Penn, founder of the Pennsylvania colony, said:

> Governments, like clocks, go from the motion men give them; and as governments are made and moved by men, so by them they are ruined too. Wherefore governments rather depend upon men than men upon governments. Let men be good and the government cannot be bad. . . . But if men be bad, let the government be never so good, they will endeavor to warp and spoil it to their turn. . . . [T]hough good laws do well, good men do better; for good laws may want [lack] good men and be abolished or invaded by ill

men; but good men will never want good laws nor suffer [allow] ill ones.[4]

We've seen this happen lots of times. We have a form of government so good that our Constitution has lasted over two hundred years, the longest-lasting republican government in the history of the world. We have known unprecedented freedom and prosperity. Yet in recent decades we've seen our wonderful governing document twisted, misapplied, misinterpreted, and lied about by men in the government. There's little wrong with our government that isn't a direct result of the people we have voted into office.

We'll wait for another chapter to deal with the court system, because it's a big enough topic in itself that we need to consider it separately from the rest of the government, but in passing let's notice that the judiciary is one of the most out-of-control facets of the government. It was bad interpretation of the Constitution that gave us the Roe v. Wade decision in 1973 that has since resulted in over 50 million abortions. It was also bad interpretation of the Constitution that has resulted in the banning of so much Christian expression from the public arena. In other words, good law — even the Constitution itself — could not protect us from bad men in places of power. We must elect good leaders. And who could God hold more accountable for that work than believers?

Here's what some of our founding fathers had to say on the importance of righteous leaders.

Noah Webster, statesman, soldier, schoolmaster, state legislator, and one of the most important contributors to the Constitution, wrote the following in his 1832 *History of the United States*:

> If the citizens neglect their duty and place unprincipled men in office, the government will soon be corrupted; laws

will be made not for the public good so much as for the selfish or local purposes. . . . If a republican government fails to secure public prosperity and happiness, it must be because the citizens neglect the divine commands, and elect bad men to make and administer the laws.[5]

John Witherspoon was one of our most accomplished founding fathers. He signed the Declaration of Independence, served on more than a hundred committees in Congress, and trained a long list of men who are also considered founders. They include 1 president, 1 vice president, 3 Supreme Court justices, 39 congressmen, 10 cabinet members, and 21 senators. This guy understood political leadership. Here's what he said about the character of the people who should be elected to office:

Those who wish well to the State ought to choose to places of trust men of inward principle, justified by exemplary conversation. Is it reasonable to expect wisdom from the ignorant? fidelity from the profligate? assiduity and application to public business from men of a dissipated life? . . . Those, therefore, who pay no regard to religion and sobriety in the persons whom they send to the legislature of any State are guilty of the greatest absurdity and will soon pay dear for their folly.[6]

Witherspoon was not one to mince words. He also said:

To promote true religion is the best and most effectual way of making a virtuous and regular people. Love to God and love to man is the substance of religion; when these prevail, civil laws will have little to do. . . . The magistrate (or ruling part of any society) ought to encourage piety . . .

[and] make it an object of public esteem. Those who are vested with civil authority ought . . . to promote religion and good morals among all their government.[7]

John Winthrop said that the best friend of liberty is one who is "most sincere and active in promoting true and undefiled religion and who sets himself with the greatest firmness to bear down on profanity and immorality of every kind."[8]

He also defined the other side of the coin: "Whoever is an avowed enemy of God, I scruple not to call him an enemy to his country."[9]

John Adams, our second president, wrote in his diary in 1772 that there was a difference between a politician and a statesman. A politician, he said, would compromise his principles to gain advantages to himself. He said that a true statesman would not compromise right and wrong because he recognized the reality of future reward and punishment — in other words, God's justice. The Reverend Chandler Robbins echoed this sentiment in an election day sermon (yes, they used to preach such things — and this was in front of Governor John Hancock and the legislature of Massachusetts) in 1791:

> Another . . . important qualification for public trust, is uncorrupted integrity — a mind free from base design — from low art and intrigue. A ruler should possess a soul above disguise, or dissimulation — that will neither be seduced by bribes and flattery, or intimidated by frowns and threatenings, to betray his trust — to counteract his judgment, or violate truth and justice.[10]

Further, Adams believed that American freedom had been founded on God's principles. In an 1813 letter to Thomas Jefferson he wrote:

The general principles upon which the Fathers achieved independence were the general principles of Christianity. . . . I will avow that I believed and now believe that those general principles of Christianity are as eternal and immutable as the existence and the attributes of God.[11]

Adams, a delegate to both the First and Second Continental Congress, vice president to George Washington, and America's negotiator of the treaty of peace with England that ended the War of Independence, was clear in his opinion that Christian morality was essential to freedom and good leadership:

Statesmen, my dear Sir, may plan and speculate for liberty, but it is religion and morality alone, which can establish the principles upon which freedom can securely stand. The only foundation of a free Constitution is pure virtue. . . . They may change their rulers and the forms of government, but they will not obtain a lasting liberty.[12]

[I]t is religion and morality alone which can establish the principles upon which freedom can securely stand. The only foundation of a free constitution is pure virtue.[13]

Others have also expressed similar thoughts:

The religion which has introduced civil liberty is the religion of Christ and His apostles, which enjoins humility, piety, and benevolence; which acknowledges in every person . . . a citizen with equal rights. This is genuine Christianity, and to this we owe our free Constitutions of Government.[14] — Noah Webster

Providence has given to our people the choice of their rulers, and it is the duty as well as the privilege and interest of our Christian nation to select and prefer Christians for their rulers.[15] — John Jay, first Chief Justice of the U.S. Supreme Court

Representative self-government stands on clear Bible principle:

Moreover you shall select from all the people able men, such as fear God, men of truth, hating covetousness; and place such over them to be rulers of thousands, rulers of hundreds, rulers of fifties, and rulers of tens (Exod. 18:21; NKJV).

So I took the heads of your tribes, wise and knowledgeable men, and made them heads over you, leaders of thousands, leaders of hundreds, leaders of fifties, leaders of tens, and officers for your tribes (Deut. 1:15; NKJV).

You shall appoint judges and officers in all your gates, which the Lord your God gives you, according to your tribes, and they shall judge the people with just judgment. You shall not pervert justice; you shall not show partiality, nor take a bribe, for a bribe blinds the eyes of the wise and twists the words of the righteous. You shall follow what is altogether just, that you may live and inherit the land which the Lord your God is giving you (Deut. 16:18–20; NKJV).

George Washington agreed with the other Founders on the issue of character in leadership. In his farewell address he said:

Of all the dispositions and habits which lead to political prosperity, religion and morality are indispensable supports. In vain would that man claim tribute to patriotism who should labor to subvert these great pillars of human happiness — these firmest props of the duties of men and citizens. . . . Reason and experience both forbid us to expect that national morality can prevail in exclusion of religious principles.[16]

So did Patrick Henry:

Virtue, morality, and religion. This is the armor, my friend, and this alone that renders us invincible. These are the tactics we should study. If we lose these, we are conquered, fallen indeed. . . . So long as our manners and principles remain sound, there is no danger.[17]

Listen to Daniel Webster, American statesman and secretary of state under three different presidents:

Lastly, our ancestors established their system of government on morality and religious sentiment. Moral habits, they believed, cannot safely be on any other foundation than religious principle, nor any government be secure which is not supported by moral habits.[18]

All these quotes may seem like overkill to prove one point, but I think we need to hit this truth hard. In our day, many people believe that personal beliefs can and should be kept separate from public life. This idea, known as compartmentalism, was what helped Bill Clinton escape conviction when he was impeached during his term as president in the 1990s. Clinton had been involved in some things that would have been considered disgraceful a generation earlier, but the idea of compartmentalism had so taken hold of the American public that his adulteries and lying under oath were excused. What he did in private was his own business, we were told. It had nothing to do with his policies as president. It didn't hurt America.

But the Bible makes it clear that nations are judged partly by the righteousness or sinfulness of their leaders. In 1 Chronicles 21, we have a clear instance of a nation suffering grave consequences because of a leader's sin:

> Then Satan stood up against Israel and moved David to number Israel. So David said to Joab and to the princes of the people, "Go, number Israel from Beersheba even to Dan, and bring me word that I may know their number." Joab said, "May the LORD add to His people a hundred times as many as they are! But, my lord the king, are they not all my lord's servants? Why does my lord seek this thing? Why should he be a cause of guilt to Israel? (1 Chron. 21:1–3).

But David insisted. Evidently he was proud of his military might or fell to the temptation of trusting to it rather than to God for protection. You'd think a guy who had killed a giant with God's help when only a lad himself would know better, but. . . .

> Nevertheless, the king's word prevailed against Joab. Therefore, Joab departed and went throughout all Israel, and came to Jerusalem. Joab gave the number of the census of all the people to David. And all Israel were 1,100,000 men who drew the sword; and Judah was 470,000 men who drew the sword (1 Chron. 21:4–5).

> God was displeased with this thing, so He struck Israel. David said to God, "I have sinned greatly, in that I have done this thing. But now, please take away the iniquity of Your servant, for I have done very foolishly" (1 Chron. 21:7–8).

> So the LORD sent a pestilence on Israel; 70,000 men of Israel fell (1 Chron. 21:14).

The head man of the country sinned and 70,000 died because of it. And yet we've bought the idea that the moral character of leaders can be separated from their political behavior.

The American church of the 20th and 21st centuries has fallen down on the job in many ways, and one of the most devastating has been our wimpy approach to the question of political leadership. It's time for a new generation of Christian warriors to take the battle to the enemy in the political arena. Did you notice in the first verse of I Chronicles 21 that it was Satan who influenced David to lead Israel into judgment? If the devil was actively attacking leaders in Old Testament times, do you really think he's not doing so today? Or is it possible he's just as busy in Washington and your state capital as he was in Jerusalem way back then?

Maybe that's why when God tells us to pray for all men, He especially calls our attention to leaders:

> First of all, then, I urge that entreaties and prayers, petitions and thanksgivings, be made on behalf of all men, for kings and all who are in authority, so that we may lead a tranquil and quiet life in all godliness and dignity. This is good and acceptable in the sight of God our Savior, who desires all men to be saved and to come to the knowledge of the truth (1 Tim. 2:1–4).

These verses tell us that we ought to pray for everybody, but especially leaders. That's the first thing we should do. I pray regularly for our current president, Barack Obama. I think he's a wicked man and I disagree with every major decision he has made in office that I'm aware of. But in the passage we just read, it says that we should pray for leaders in order that we can live a quiet and tranquil life. That sounds good to me. Besides, verse 4 tells us that God "desires all men to be saved and come to the knowledge of the truth." That includes Barack Obama, and despite the fact that I believe he has done great harm to American freedom, I have no desire for him to go to hell. I don't wish that on anybody. Besides, far better for him to get saved, publicly renounce his former beliefs, and turn his administration around. What a blow for Christ and freedom that would be.

If we lived in a monarchy like the Old Testament Israelites, we couldn't do much besides prayer in order to influence leadership. But in America, there is much we can do. Remember, we are all the "king" here. We'll talk more about the specific things we can do later in the chapter. For now, I hope we can agree that we are supposed to be doing *something*.

Okay, let's summarize. What I've been trying to do in this chapter so far is to establish a few basic ideas that we all need to understand and be committed to. Not necessarily in chronological order, they are:

- America is in big trouble and much of the trouble stems from government;
- We the People are in fact the government and the people we vote into office are just our representatives;
- God's blessing, resulting in the peace and prosperity of the country, depends on the character of the leaders we elect;
- The American nation was established on the biblical principle of congregational rule through representative government; in other words, a republic;
- Christians have a profound responsibility to influence government toward righteousness through prayer, the electoral process, and other means.

Your Challenge

What does all this mean to you — you, the homeschooled student or graduate, coming of age in a time when our culture has degenerated and is producing both leaders and followers who are ignorant of God's ways and careless of His standards?

It means you are the answer to the last generation's prayers. And it means that you need to get busy fighting God's battles in the public arena. Now, not later. Don't protest to me that you're only 12 or 13. Don't tell me that you'll get started as soon as you're done with your education or get married and settled down. Don't tell me that you'll start as soon as you get your career off the ground. And above all, don't tell me you're having too much fun right now and just can't be bothered with taking on adult responsibility yet. That kind of talk gets all over my last nerve.

The first thing is to prepare yourself. Of course, the most important preparation is spiritual. You're supposed to be taking care of that already through your parents' teaching, your personal prayer life and Bible study, and your church involvement. Just remember that God won't bless your natural efforts at reformation if you're not putting spiritual things first.

Beyond staying close to the Lord — staying "blessable" as one preacher says — inform yourself about the battle in government. You need to learn what the Constitution says and how it should be applied to life in America so that you can see where it's being perverted and oppose it. How do you get informed? I'm glad you asked.

First, *read*. Read books by authors you trust. If you don't know what books to read, ask people you respect what they recommend on the subject. Read the writings of the founders, available at any library. People like Franklin, Washington, Jefferson,

Madison, Adams, and most of the other leading men of their day wrote voluminously and their writings aren't hard to find. You can read a lot of them online for free at websites such as the one maintained by Project Gutenberg. They have over 30,000 free e-books you can read any time you like. People whom I respect recommend also *Democracy in America* by Alexis de Tocqueville.

Also, read the *Federalist Papers*. This is a book compiled of writings of founding fathers James Madison, Alexander Hamilton, and John Jay. It was originally a series of articles written by the three men to urge the 13 new states, formerly English colonies, to ratify the new American Constitution. It is the recognized authority for what the Constitution really means and intends. You need to know the Constitution, because it is the foundation of America. It "constitutes" our government. Everybody in evangelical circles claims to believe in the Constitution. But it's rather like the Bible in that everybody refers to it to justify their opinions; everybody claims to revere it, but nobody reads it. How many Christians have read every chapter of the Bible? How many American citizens have read every page of the Constitution? It's a short document, amounting to only about 20 pages in a book like this. Yet few of us have read it from start to finish, even though it is the document that secures our basic human rights.

The founders had just come through a war for freedom when they wrote the Constitution. They well understood how important it was for free men to know how freedom works. John Adams said,

> Children should be educated and instructed in the principles of freedom.[19]

Why would he think that's so important? Because he knew that when people don't understand their freedom, they don't take it seriously. And when they don't take it seriously, they don't protect it. And when they don't protect it, governments take it away from them. In our time, the Constitution has been misused by some in government to reduce our freedom rather than protect it, and this succeeds only because so many Americans don't know what it says and so fail to hold their leaders accountable to respect it.

> The Constitution is not an instrument for the government to restrain the people, it is an instrument for the people to restrain the government. — attributed to Patrick Henry

Read the Constitution and read about it. Then read other stuff that will help you learn how to protect, support, and defend it all your life. You will soon learn, if you don't know it already, that there are many people who are twisting it all the time in order to take your freedom away from you. President Franklin D. Roosevelt, a pioneer in misinterpreting the Constitution in order to increase government and restrict freedom, said:

> The United States Constitution has proved itself the most marvelously elastic compilation of rules of government ever written.[20]

Isn't that encouraging? He thought that the document that guarantees your right to freedom of religion, freedom of speech, freedom of the press, freedom from unlawful search and seizure — is *elastic*! Do you want the protections of your freedom to be elastic? I don't. I want them to be solid as the Rock of Gibraltar. The incredible thing about this quote is that it came from a speech he made as governor of New York in 1930, expounding the idea of state's and individual's rights rather than the powers of the federal government. Just two years later he was elected president and began the greatest attack on those very constitutional principles that has ever been launched. Here is a potent warning about the need to look at a candidate's character as well as his stated beliefs. Roosevelt went from pontificating on the virtues of limited government to radically expanding government in an amazingly short time. Apparently he considered the Constitution "elastic" in a very different way than one would gather from the 1930 speech. There are far more people in America who think Roosevelt's way now than there were in his own lifetime, so know your Constitution and be prepared to protect it against misinterpretation.

There are some great political websites, including those of the Heritage Foundation, the Cato Institute, Atlas Economic Research Foundation, and the Avalon Project. At many such sites you can read tons of articles and purchase books as well. My favorite website is Wallbuilders.com, operated by Christian historian David Barton, a personal hero of mine and a man I believe has been specifically raised up by God to help restore America's Christian heritage.

There are some periodic publications you will find helpful. Among these are *Conservative Chronicle* (reprinted articles by conservative thinkers that I read every week), *Human Events,* and *National Review.* You can probably get sample copies by contacting them through their websites. If not, ask around at church and see if anybody has old copies you can borrow. This will introduce you to many different writers and publications so you'll learn which to listen to and which to disregard.

The "mainstream media," meaning most television news and most of the big newspapers, are usually controlled by people who do not think biblically or constitutionally, so take anything you see or hear from those sources with a large grain of salt. I glance at the headlines as I pass a newspaper box occasionally, but I've learned that there's usually much more accurate news and commentary available through other sources, so I seldom read further than a quick perusal of the front page.

A lot of your education comes informally from people you hang around with, so pick your companions carefully. I think you'll find, though, that some of that comes automatically. If you choose to spend your spare time doing things that matter (rather than, say, striving to become paintball champion of the world), you will usually find yourself in the company of people who talk about things that matter. Next time campaign season comes around, pick a worthy candidate and work to get him elected. You'll find that most of the people who bother to come out and work for him are people you can learn good things from. Reading, working, building relationships — it all works together to build a better "you."

You can acquire a lot of your education in pretty simple, informal settings. You're a fortunate person if dinnertime conversation at your house centers around things of eternal importance. If it does, no doubt you've already learned a lot about how America works and how blessed we are to live here. If it doesn't, make it a point to mention during the meal something you've been reading about and get the perspective of your parents and siblings about it. There's a lot of benefit in the informal batting of ideas back and forth across the dinner table. Ronald Reagan said, "All great change in America begins at the dinner table."[21] If you can think of a person who knows a lot that you want to know, get your parents to invite him to supper. Be ready with a few questions to get him talking and be prepared to shut up and absorb.

This is something that Benjamin Franklin's father used to do, primarily for the purpose of educating his children. Judging by Ben's career, he had a wise father. As Longfellow said, "A single conversation across the table with a wise man is better than ten years' mere study with books."[22] That's the value of informal conversation.

Remember, we're coming from the assumption that leadership is the key to reforming a society. So as we approach the problem of government, we look at it through that lens. Actually, government should be one area in which it's easy to see the leadership structure and the effects it has, because government is essentially a leadership system. In America, it's elected leadership rather than leadership by force, but it's leadership all the same. We send our representatives to Washington, our state capitals, and city hall by popular vote in the expectation that they will provide us with leadership that reflects the fact that they are supposed to represent the will of the majority.

There are two main problems in the system. The first is that the leaders we get are no better than the voters who elect them. Since three out of every four evangelicals who are eligible to vote don't bother to do so, electing leaders is left up to people who are much less likely to fear God and respect His principles. The second problem is that there exists a cadre of unelected people who have power that should only belong to elected representatives. The most prominent class of this group would be the judges of the court system, who frequently frustrate the clear will of the voters by overturning laws passed by the people's representatives. A state legislature or the U.S. Congress can pass a law that is very popular with the electorate, only to have the Supreme Court come along and say, "Nope. That's unconstitutional. Can't do it." And the people are back to square one.

We'll deal with the judiciary in a later chapter because it's such a big issue all by itself. Suffice it to say for now that judges are either elected by a vote of the people, or appointed by people who are elected. So elective politics is important.

Now let's talk about the leadership *you* will bring to the table. There are an awful lot of Christians who think they have done their duty to the country by voting. In fact, there's a myth going around — maybe you've heard it — about "being involved in the process." In other words, it doesn't matter for whom you vote, as long as you've done your duty by making a choice and pulling the lever at the ballot box.

Saying that it doesn't matter how you vote just as long as you voted makes about as much sense as saying it doesn't matter who you shoot, just as long as you've shot. Just take part in the process. Doesn't matter whom you marry, just get married. Be involved.

Personally, I wish people who either don't bother to get informed on the issues first, or who are going to vote for whoever promises to give them what they want without regard to what's right or constitutional, would just stay out of the voting booth. There are far too many people who vote strictly by party affiliation or by a "what's-in-it-for-me" attitude, and that's a big part of the problem we have in government. That's what Noah Webster meant where I quoted him earlier in this chapter: "If the citizens neglect their duty and place unprincipled men in office, the government will soon be corrupted; laws will be made not for the public good so much as for the selfish or local purposes."

What are selfish or local purposes? It's a selfish purpose when a politician votes for a bill that will please rich people who contribute big bucks to his re-election campaign. It's a local purpose when your congressman supports a bill that will benefit your district — keeping his constituents happy so he can keep his job — at the expense of the rest of the country.

There was a great example of both selfish and local purposes just a few years ago in a project that came to be facetiously called

"The Bridge to Nowhere." It was proposed to build a huge bridge from Ketchikan, Alaska, to Gravina Island, which was home to an international airport but only 50 residents. The island is currently served by a ferry boat that runs every 30 minutes most of the year and every 15 minutes during peak traffic seasons. The ferry ride costs five dollars. And what was the federal government's idea to replace the ferry? A gigantic structure, nearly as long as the Golden Gate Bridge and taller than the Brooklyn Bridge, with a price tag of $398 million. To reach an island where 50 people live.

The project was energetically supported by, among others, Alaska Senator Ted Stevens, who was prosecuted for corruption in 2008 (for matters not related to the bridge). Why would a politician support such a ridiculous measure? Because it would have resulted in the expenditure of almost half a billion dollars in his state with the bill paid by the American taxpayer. It would have provided jobs for tons of workers and sales for tons of businesses, all paying taxes in Alaska. It would have made his constituents — Alaska voters — very happy with him. But it would have amounted in fact to robbing the rest of the country to produce these benefits for one state. That is a selfish and local interest. Similar things are done every day in governments at the local, state, and national level. And that's why we're paying out nearly half of our income as citizens in taxes.

We need to reform and replace leadership in the political realm, and that's the task for your generation. Some of you will be presidents, congressmen, and senators. Others of you will be parents of such people. All of you should be involved in electing them.

You say, but wait a minute. I'm too young to vote. I'm only 15. What can I do? Good question. The kind that's easy to answer.

Okay, you're 15. How many votes will you have in the next election? None, you say? Wrong answer. *You have as many votes as you can influence.* Let's say you have a friend who's 18. If he's not planning on voting and you talk him into voting for your favorite candidate, you have essentially cast one vote. If your buddy was planning on voting for your man's opponent and you persuade him to vote for your guy instead, you have just cast two votes because you have added one to your candidate's tally AND subtracted one from the opponent's. Maybe one or both of your parents failed to get around to voting last time. If you remind them ahead of time and that gets them into the booth next election day, you have added two votes to somebody's tally. And if you are old enough to vote, you can *double* your value by convincing just one other person to vote your way.

Another thing you can do at 15 — or much younger — is to work the polls on election day. Pick a candidate you believe supports the Constitution, get in touch with his campaign, and arrange to be at the polling place for a designated time slot on the big day, passing out his literature and asking people to vote for him. Every four years there is an election for president, every six years for the Senate, every two years for Congress. Believe it or not, a small percentage of voters actually come to the polls without their minds made up as to which candidate to pick for the presidency or Congress (totally uninformed but dutifully being "involved in the process"). These people will, for the most part, make up their minds based on what they see and hear at the polling place.

There is a much larger group of voters who come with their minds made up about the presidential or congressional election and know little or nothing about other things that may be lower on the ballot. For instance, most state, city, and county legislatures elect their candidates on the same dates as the federal elections. Also, there are often referenda — plural for referendum — on the ballot at the same time. A referendum could involve a tax increase, zoning issue, or some other change that could seriously affect the lives of people in the community. Such issues as these don't get nearly the publicity that the national elections do, so many voters come to the polls unprepared to cast a responsible vote. They need poll workers to inform them.

Another reason poll workers are critical to the elective process is this: most people who get elected to high office have been elected to lower office first. That means that the guy running for city council in a town of five thousand inhabitants may be running for the U.S. Congress in just a few years. It's like farm teams in baseball. Guys play on minor league teams owned by the New York Yankees or the Boston Red Sox, sometimes for several years, and eventually some of them prove themselves good enough to be promoted to the major league. Farm teams are also sometimes called feeder clubs.

So it is in elective politics. Rarely do you hear of a guy going to Congress or the Senate who has never been elected to a lower office such as town council, school board, or county clerk. That's where most people get their first legislative experience. And that's why it's important for you to know who's the "good guy" in each of these lower races and support him. Someday soon he may be in the state legislature voting on laws about homeschooling, right-to-life issues, etc. And maybe even in Washington.

So work the polls for your candidate or issue. No, you're not too young. Our family all works on election day. My youngest daughter, Kasey, was campaigning for our congressman, Virgil Goode, one election day when she was nine years old. She saw a man drive up and get out of a pickup truck. Noticing the truck and the fact that he was wearing camo clothes, she judged him to be a hunter. Walking briskly up to him before he even had a chance to approach the building, she said, "Do you like to hunt?" A bit surprised, he said, "Well, yes, I do." She handed him a flyer. "Well, if you want to keep your guns, you'd better vote for Virgil Goode." As he exited the building a few minutes later he gave her a grin and said, "I voted for your man."

People certainly won't always vote the way you want them too, but there is no doubt they are impressed with a young person who is respectful, confident, neatly dressed, and without a lot of tattoos and shrapnel-plugged perforations (also known as piercings).

You also need to be looking around in your circle of acquaintances for people who would be good community leaders. It may be that someone you know at church would make a good candidate. The best leaders are those who aren't interested in power for themselves, so it may be that a great prospect isn't even thinking about running for office. Maybe you should prayerfully offer a suggestion to someone like that. And maybe you should be praying about such a future move for yourself.

> Instead of giving a politician the keys to the city, it might be better to change the locks.[23] — Doug Larson

How to Influence Legislators at the State and National Level

In America, we have a "bicameral" Congress. That means that "Congress" is divided into two houses — the House of Representatives and the Senate. For the purposes of this chapter, I will refer to your congressman, but for the most part, I will mean your senator or congressman, or your state legislator, and generally, the same rules apply to influencing any of the three.

Since there are two senators for each state regardless of the population, they represent a much larger geographical area and population than does each congressman. They are correspondingly more difficult to influence, as your individual voice is competing with a large number of other voices. In my state of Virginia, for instance, there are 11 congressional districts, with one representative in each. So we have over five times as many congressmen as senators. That means that, statistically, the two senators are about five times as difficult to influence, at least on the basis of how many other constituents they have to listen to besides me.

It sounds like a nearly impossible job to get the ear of a national legislator and influence his votes, but it's not as difficult as it seems. For one thing, only a very few of the citizens in a congressional district ever make any serious attempt to contact their representative. So you're not competing with anywhere near everybody in your district. In addition, there is the cumulative effect of hearing from the same person or group year after year. Those people are remembered and respected. Others may write a letter or turn out to vote on one issue that is important to them, but then disappear into the woodwork after that issue is settled. They don't carry as much weight as those who are heard from year after year, issue after issue, election after election. That's you.

How Laws Are Passed in Congress

After a senator or representative introduces a bill, it is assigned to the appropriate committee, according to subject area, for markup. Here it is studied and rewritten. Hearings are held to solicit both public and special-interest views.

During markup, the committee considers the specific language of a bill and may amend or change it. When the bill clears the committee, it goes to the floor for general debate and action.

Once both houses pass a bill, a conference committee made up of both senators and representatives works out any differences between the House-passed and Senate-passed versions.

The final conference version must be approved by both houses, then the bill goes to the president to be signed into law. The president may veto the bill. In that case, a two-thirds veto override vote in both houses is required for the bill to become law.

When to Lobby

At any point in this process you may want to personally lobby your representative, senators, the House and Senate leaders, or the president. There are special times in the legislative process when your letters and calls can be especially productive.

Party Time

Speaking of where candidates come from, it's crucial for you to be actively involved in a political party. I haven't always believed that; in fact, I used to have a major objection to party membership. I figured the thing to do was to vote for the best candidate regardless of party affiliation. If he was worthy of leadership, he wouldn't let his party influence him in the wrong way.

Then I got mugged by reality. With time and experience, I learned that political parties are simply groups of people organized around values they hold in common. Of course they don't all agree on everything, but they have enough shared beliefs that they are distinctly different from other groups who share a different list of beliefs. So people who believe in certain things join together to work toward the advancement of their goals. There's nothing wrong with that; it's the logical way to get things done. The right or wrong of it comes in the beliefs they share and the goals they're advancing.

Another potential wrong is the very common tendency to be more loyal to one's party than to God, America, or the Constitution. Plenty of people join the party they believe will do the most for them, regardless of what damage its policies may do to others. I'm sure I don't have to tell you that's wrong.

Because most politically active people do organize themselves into large groups (parties), it is nearly impossible to make major changes in the political direction of the local, state, or federal government without a party's cooperation. That's reality, so don't think you can be strictly "independent" and get much accomplished. Just always remember that party loyalty is never cause to compromise truth.

Keep a healthy awareness of the dangers of party spirit. George Washington said:

> They [parties] serve to organize faction, to give it an artificial and extraordinary force; to put, in the place of the delegated will of the nation, the will of a party, often a small but artful and enterprising minority of the community.[24]

Always stand firm in what you believe, jealously guarding your core values from the influence of those in the same party, even if they're the majority. Listen to Thomas Jefferson:

> I never submitted the whole system of my opinions to the creed of any party of men whatever, in religion, in philosophy, in politics, or in anything else, where I was capable of thinking for myself. Such an addiction is the last degradation of a free and moral agent.[25]

So with those cautions in mind, I encourage you to join a party and push for your values, both in government and in the party itself.

Which Party?

As you know, the Republicans and the Democrats are the two main political parties in America. There are several other parties, but to date none of them are large enough to seriously compete with these two on a national level. So if you want to make a significant change in the direction of the country any time in the near future (which I most certainly do) you should join one of these two. Take time to be informed about their platforms and make the choice for yourself. I am a member of the Republican Party and that is what I strongly recommend to you. I'll tell you why I chose the Republicans over the Democrats in just a minute, but first let me explain why I don't think you should choose from one of the other options.

Those other options are called third parties. I know it sounds weird since you logically can't have more than one "third" place on any list, but that's the jargon that's developed. There are three "third" parties that boast over 100,000 registered members. These are the Green Party (emphasizing environmental issues), the Libertarian Party (conservative in many respects, but far off base on moral issues like abortion and gay marriage), and the Constitution Party.

The Constitution Party, formerly the U.S. Taxpayers Party, was founded by Mr. Howard Phillips, father of my good buddy Doug Phillips. Mr. Phillips is one of the smartest men I've ever met, a great Christian and a great American. The party platform is wonderful, honoring God and the Constitution. Many of my friends in the homeschooling movement belong to the Constitution Party. It has grown considerably since its establishment in 1992, but still its membership is only a fraction of either of the two major parties.

There are a number of other third parties, too, some appealing and some appalling. Because of their numerical inferiority, their candidates rarely get elected. Currently, only 2 of the 100 U.S. Senators, Bernie Sanders and Joe Lieberman, are third party people, and Lieberman was originally elected as a Democrat.

The reason that I chose the Republican Party over the Democrats is that the creed (philosophy) of the Republicans is much closer to my own. I believe in the right to life, religious freedom, limited government, original intent of the Constitution, a restrained judiciary, parents' rights, a strong national defense, educational freedom, low taxes, and a host of other positions normally referred to as *conservative*. The Republican Party's official stance is very much in line with what I believe. Right now the higher party leadership has drifted seriously from those ideas, but I'm involved in a grassroots movement to set them straight, which I hope you will be a part of in the near future. To explain what the party officially stands for, despite the failures of some in leadership today, read the Republican Creed:

We Believe:

That the free enterprise system is the most productive supplier of human needs and economic justice,

That all individuals are entitled to equal rights, justice, and opportunities and should assume their responsibilities as citizens in a free society,

That fiscal responsibility and budgetary restraints must be exercised at all levels of government,

That the Federal Government must preserve individual liberty by observing Constitutional limitations,

That peace is best preserved through a strong national defense,

That faith in God, as recognized by our Founding Fathers, is essential to the moral fiber of the Nation.

Now let me explain why I chose the Republican Party over any of the other parties, even though one or more of them might be even closer to my philosophy than the Republicans. The reason is simply that none of the third parties is in a position to save this country. Why? Because they're too small and weak and it takes time to grow a party that can compete at the national level. I don't believe we have time for that. We're too far gone. Our government has gradually taken on far too much power over the citizens and that is tyranny. Since the election of Barack Obama, whose policies appear to be those of a radical Socialist, the decay has gone much faster. With the Democratic Party in control of the Senate, the House of Representatives, and the White House for the first two years of the Obama administration, government invasion into our private lives and businesses rolled like a tidal wave. In February of 2009, the month following President Obama's inauguration, Newsweek Magazine crowed, "We Are All Socialists Now." That's a radical statement to be made by a national publication in a free republic. The fact that it didn't create a firestorm of public outrage is a symptom of how far we've come from the founders' ideals of liberty. They must be rolling in their graves.

The Democrats are in favor of this Socialist progression. None of the third parties is close to having the muscle to stop it. I believe the only practical move is to reform the Republican Party and use it to move our government back in the right direction. Some of my friends say that the Republicans are too far gone as well; that the Democrats are destroying our freedom faster, but that the Republicans are just taking us over the same cliff at a slower pace. They say we don't have enough power to win the party elections we'd need to win in order to reform and replace leadership. To that I say, if Christian conservatives can't muster enough votes to win an election in the party, how in the world can we muster enough to win in the general public? In other words, if we can't put together a majority in the Republican Party, how can we leave it, form a third party, and garner enough votes to win a general election with two major parties against us? It doesn't add up.

To me, the only thing that makes sense is to reform one of the two major parties. And the Republicans are light years closer to being reformed than the Democrats. But before we leave the subject, let me give you an illustration about why I don't think a third party is the way to go at this time in history.

Imagine that you're a nobleman in medieval times, say, a baron. You live in a huge castle that has been your family's home for generations. It took a hundred years to build and it is a strong, solid fortification. Any enemy would think twice about trying to breach its thick stone walls and conquer you.

But somehow, over a long period of time it is infiltrated. Distant family members move in, one or two at a time, so quietly that at first you hardly notice the newcomers. After all, it's a "big tent"; there's room for everybody in the clan. But then you begin to notice that the new folks seem to be growing in numbers and the closer family to be decreasing. There are some dominant types among the newbies who begin to make their opinions known. The new members begin to demand better seats at the table and gobble up more of the groceries than you're comfortable with. You begin to feel a bit uncomfortable with the changing complexion of the clan.

Then one night there's a big revolt and the next thing you know, *wham!* You've just been tossed in the dungeon and somebody else is running the castle. You're told that you'll be allowed out of the dungeon and can even sit at the table, way down at the far end where it's drafty. Or you can move out and go it on your own. What do you do?

You have a choice. You can submit, sit quietly at the drafty end of the table, and eat whatever is left when the serving bowls finally get to you. Or you can move out and build a new castle; but that takes a hundred years. I would choose a different route. I would win over everybody at my end of the table, invite lots of my friends to come in as well, and when I had enough people in my corner I'd jolly well stage an uprising and take my castle back.

Something like this process has happened in the Republican Party. Years ago it was the province of constitutional conservatives. In 1980 we nominated Ronald Reagan for president; he won and became one of the best presidents of the 20th century, as well as one of the most popular. Conservatives were in the places of leadership and the party took a conservative stance on issues and candidates. But slowly that changed. Bit by bit some conservatives became less conservative and more and more people joined the party who were less conservative already. That's to be expected, considering the general population has grown less conservative, thanks to government education. So as the older Republican leadership died off, younger folks who were generally less constitutional in their philosophies replaced them. And of course, those who were most motivated to change the party were the most vocal and tended to grow in influence. Christian conservatives found themselves at the drafty end of the dining room. Somebody else was in charge.

What shall we do? Take a hundred years and build another party? If we do, we'll have two major parties to oppose us. Besides, our country has gone so far in a bad direction that I don't believe we'll last another hundred years in freedom if we don't reform one of the major political parties quickly. No, the thing to do is fix the leadership problem in the Republican Party. We do that by reforming some leaders and replacing others. If we replace enough, many others will reform themselves. But how do we go about this reforming and replacing? I'll give you a real-life example.

My family's involvement in politics began not with me but with my eldest son, whose name is also Rick. He's not a Junior, but that's a long story best saved for another time. Anyway, he got interested in politics while still a little guy, in fact, when Reagan was running for president and Rickey was 6 years old. At 16, Rick began working as a volunteer for the Republican Party in Campbell County, Virginia, where we have lived for many years. At first, all he could do was stuff envelopes, make phone calls, and go out with teams putting up campaign signs. But he became fascinated with the political process and had developed some very strong political opinions already. So he got more and more involved with the county party, and at age 19 got elected chairman, one of the youngest county party chairmen in the history of the Virginia Republican Party.

Rick is the kind of guy who throws himself intensely into everything he does that he considers important, so the amount of knowledge he accumulated in his first three years in the party was very impressive. In fact, Pat McSweeney, the chairman of the Republican Party of Virginia, called Rick "a self-taught political genius" in an interview with *Virginia Business* magazine. At the same time, Rick's hard work was paying off in a rising tide of new conservative Christians becoming involved in the party. That included his parents and each of his siblings as they came of voting age. In fact, Rick's siblings have also become integrally involved in the party in their own right. Rick was elected to a second term as chairman two years later, despite a hard-fought challenge from the more liberal (statist) wing of the party. A few months into his second term, Rick accepted a scholarship to attend Liberty University. He resigned the chair in order to give full attention to school and work, but when the special election was held to replace him, he had organized his forces and was successful in getting another Christian conservative elected to the spot.

I can't resist inserting a note here that after finishing his degree in three years, Rick ran for a seat on the Campbell County Board of Supervisors and won. Part of the delicious irony of the situation was that the incumbent he ousted was a "visiting teacher" for the school system. That means truant officer. Another part of it was the fact that the same school superintendent who had prosecuted our family for homeschooling some 20 years before was still in that position. That meant that my kid, who once hid under the bed from that gentleman, now had the opportunity to vote on his school budget each year. Gotta love the irony.

During all these years, Rick had been working on recruiting new conservatives into the party. Not only that, he had also been building relationships with conservative leaders in the local parties of the surrounding counties and helping them recruit good new members into their party units. So a conservative wave (mostly Christians) was growing throughout a several-county area in central Virginia. That wave culminated in 2010 in a long-sought-after goal: a majority of the county party chairs in our congressional district were occupied by conservatives.

Your eyes may be glazing over a bit at this point, so let me explain why all this organizational talk is important. Simply put, the chairmen of the local party units in a congressional district have a huge influence on who will be the party's candidate for Congress in the next election. That is a very big deal.

In Virginia, the Republican Party is organized by state, district, and local units. There is the Republican Party of Virginia, the state party. There are the city and county parties, the local units. These local units are grouped together into the congressional districts. We live in the Fifth Congressional District, so our Campbell County Republican Party is a unit in the Fifth. The leadership committee of the Fifth District party consists mostly of the chairmen of the 21 city and county units in the district, along with a couple of members of the Virginia Republican Party ruling committee.

Wow, even my eyes are glazing over after rereading that last paragraph. So here's the punch line: in the local party elections of 2010, we got enough conservatives elected as county chairmen that we finally have a solid majority on the Fifth District Republican committee. One of those chairmen is Rick's brother Nate, who now chairs the party in neighboring Bedford County. Another of Rick's brothers, Tim, was elected vice chairman of the Fifth District party. Meanwhile, the boys and their crew helped out with some other conservative campaigns, including that of their friend Daniel Bradshaw, who was elected chairman of the Prince Edward County unit. Daniel is a homeschool graduate, 18 years old at the time of his election. As it happened, the first election for him as a candidate. So much for the common criticism that homeschooled kids lack socialization.

I know the organizational structure I've described here may not be clear to you, and it may be that the Republican Party in your state is set up differently. But the principle is the same: elect enough of the right people to leadership at the local level and before too long they will rise to higher levels of leadership, replacing people who are less loyal to constitutional principles. Grassroots Christian activism, led largely by homeschooled young people, has been very successful in the Fifth District of Virginia. In fact I believe it is now safe to say that if Christian homeschoolers don't like a certain candidate, he will have a very hard time winning the Republican nomination for the next election for Congress. That's huge.

I am not saying that the newly conservative flavor of the Republican Party leadership in our district is exclusively due to the activism of my kids. Far from it; they have had tons of help from people they have mentored, and much mentoring from more experienced people from both inside and outside the district. But the fact of the matter is that conservative Christians, recruited from many local churches and led by graduates of homeschooling families, have had a gigantic impact on the district party and therefore on congressional elections for the foreseeable future. If it can be done here, it can be done in your district. It can be done everywhere in the country. And the best part is, we don't have to lead every congressional district. We just have to lead in a majority of them and we already have a lot.

I hope that you'll join us in reforming the Republican Party from the grassroots up. America is still a "center-right" country, meaning that on average we're more conservative than liberal. That means that if the Republicans put forth more conservative candidates, we either win the elections or force the Democrats to put forth more conservative people to beat us. Either way, the Constitution wins. Freedom wins.

Endnotes

1. http://www.quotedb.com/quotes/3669.
2. http://baptistbrethren.com/america/the-time-has-come.
3. Ibid.
4. http://explorepahistory.com/odocument.php?docId=1-4-23D.
5. Noah Webster, *History of the United States* (New Haven, CT: Durrie & Peck, 1832), p. 336–337.
6. http://www.partyof1776.net/p1776/fathers/Witherspoon%20John/quotes/contents.html.
7. http://vftonline.org/EndTheWall/promote.htm.
8. Speech at Princeton, May 17, 1776, http://www.allaboutworldview.org/christian-politics.htm.
9. Ibid.
10. http://www.wallbuilders.com/LIBissuesArticles.asp?id=4157.
11. http://christianity.about.com/od/independenceday/a/foundingfathers.htm.
12. http://www.liberty1.org/virtue.htm.
13. http://www.liberty1.org/virtue.htm.
14. www.whateveristrue.com/heritage/ofathers.htm.

15. http://en.wikipedia.org/wiki/John_Jay.

16. http://www.crossroad.to/text/articles/WashingtonFarewell.html.

17. http://www.davidstuff.com/usa/henry2.htm.

18. http://www.historicrichlandchurch.org/page3/page3.html.

19. http://thoughtsonquotes.blogspot.com/2007/11/freedom-survives-through-our-children.html.

20. http://www.lexrex.com/enlightened/writings/fdr_address.htm.

21. http://old.nationalreview.com/document/reagan200406052132.asp.

22. http://www.brainyquote.com/quotes/quotes/h/henrywadsw138607.html.

23. http://www.1-famous-quotes.com/quote/325047.

24. http://www.laughtergenealogy.com/bin/history/politics.html.

25. http://www.britannica.com/presidents/article-9116912.

Chapter 6

EDUCATION

"The hand that rocks the cradle rules the world."

It's a very old saying and it simply means that whoever controls the upbringing of children controls the future. The children are the future. If we are to have a good, decent, orderly, and responsible society, we must train up good, decent, orderly, responsible children. That is the kind of adults they will someday be. If we end up with another kind of society 20 years from now, it will be because we have trained up a different kind of children.

From the time of our founding — even before — it was understood that the training of children was the responsibility of the parents. It was taken seriously and it worked. Solid families built a solid society. So solid, in fact, that when the British government tried to meddle in the rights of families, they found out what a solid society, indeed, had been built. Their bullying resulted in the loss of their American colonies and a new nation was born.

With our new freedom, we Americans proceeded to amaze the rest of the world with what free people can do. We were constantly coming up with new advances in technology, science, politics, literature, and community life. We were free to dream — for ourselves and our children — and we did dream. We taught our kids that they could accomplish great things and be great people. We had freedom, so there was nothing but our own attitudes to hold us back.

Along with freedom comes responsibility, and we taught that to our children as well. Few families owned many books, but nearly all had a Bible and they read it often. Except for the frontier areas, the moral temperature of communities was high. People had respect for themselves and each other, for the Bible taught that. America worked.

But from early in our history there had been seeds sown of a different way of thinking, a philosophy that today we call statism or socialism. This idea said that it wasn't best for families to be independent. It said that they should share property, with someone outside the family deciding who should share what with whom, how much of it and under what circumstances it should be shared. People couldn't be trusted with too much freedom.

The Pilgrims had experimented with socialism the first year or two. They shared land and crops, expecting that everyone would contribute what they could to the colony's storehouses and take back what they needed. It didn't work, as it has never worked anywhere it has been tried, though it's been tried all over the world for centuries. People are just more motivated to take care of themselves and their families than they are to work for the benefit of some vague concept called society.

So socialism was a brief experiment in the early colonies. Free enterprise and private property worked, as Scripture indicates. It's best for every man to have his own vine and fig tree.

But the idea of socialism was alive and well in other places. America hadn't heard the last of it. While still a young country, America saw socialism again. One of its most notable appearances came in the 1820s in the form of an experiment called New Harmony.

New Harmony was a settlement in what is now the state of Indiana, on the fertile ground along the banks of the Wabash River. It was established by a wealthy Englishman, Robert Owen, who seemed to have something of a messiah complex. Owen was a philanthropist who had spent much of his considerable fortune in efforts to help the poor. In his wool carding mills in Scotland he had created a whole village to which poor people could come, work in the mills, and raise their children in his village. Casting an interested eye on the new nation called America, he thought he saw good soil for a larger experiment in communal living. So he bought hundreds of acres of land from a settlement of German immigrants, rented out portions to families, and began to try to train his people to believe in shared property.

It didn't work any better for the Owenites in the 1820s than it had for the Pilgrims in the 1620s. People just didn't try as hard when the fruit of their labors had to be shared with others outside their families — some of whom might not have worked quite as hard as it was felt that they should. But despite the fact that his "warm and fuzzy" experiment had failed, Owen was not deterred. He thought he knew what the problem was and how to fix it. It would just take more time.

Robert Owen and his followers concluded that Americans were just too fractious to be sociable. They had lived lives of independence for too many generations to see the beauty of socialist living. What was to be done? Get a grip on them while they were children and train them up rightly. American adults were incorrigible capitalists.

The Owenite movement gave up for the moment on the commune idea and went to work in dead earnest on public education. They established a newspaper in New York City called the *Free Inquirer*. It was nothing more than an offspring of the defunct *New Harmony Gazette*. Along with its sister publication in Philadelphia, the *Mechanics' Free Press*, it was a mouthpiece for Owenism. Their main issue was educational reform.

The Owenites eventually found an ally. The early Unitarians were another group dedicated to reforming society. Unitarianism had crossed the Atlantic in the 1600s and taken root in Boston. Boston had traditionally been a hotbed of Calvinism, the religion of the original founders of the colony. But the Unitarian doctrine of the innate goodness of man was attractive to many people and grew to the point that, after a contest of a century, Unitarians were successful in taking over famous Harvard University, originally formed to train preachers of the gospel.

Unitarians had different beliefs than the atheistic Owenites, but they shared a common interest in the education of children. Owen had concluded that the training of children must be taken away from parents so that they wouldn't grow up to be evil, selfish capitalists. The Unitarians also believed that children must be trained by someone other than their (mostly Calvinist) parents because of the doctrine of original sin. They believed that it was because children were taught that they were sinners that they grew up acting like sinners. Sinning.

So the Owenites thought that the enemy was capitalism while the Unitarians thought the enemy was the doctrine of sin. Both agreed, however, on what needed to be done. The two groups came to the same conclusion as would Karl Marx and Friedrich Engels decades later when they were smoking dope together in Germany.

If they wanted to recreate society, they had to get the training of children out of the family, out of the Church, and into the public arena where they could get control of it.

That was a long time ago. The Owenites and Unitarians, along with other social engineers long ago, succeeded in persuading government to make "public" education the law of the land. Now millions of school children provide a captive audience to those who want to hawk their philosophies to the upcoming generation. The system reflects its Unitarian heritage in the teaching of situational ethics or "values clarification." The Owenite influence can be seen in the Socialist approach to economics (in some classrooms, children are told to buy their crayons, bring them to school, and put them in a "common" basket to be shared with all). Over the years, plenty of other groups and businesses have come to have a stake in the juicy prospect of millions of kids, sitting in their desks and waiting to be told what to do, what to read, and what to think.

It would be natural to assume that our national system of public education came into existence as a response to a general need for education. That is not true. From very early in our history — including colonial times — Americans were competent at educating their children. Studies have shown literacy in the colonies at the time of the War of Independence to be nearly 100 percent among the non-slave population. Some parents taught their children at home, some hired tutors, communities often combined resources and established local schools. All was under local control. Because no one could be forced to go to school prior to compulsory attendance (a comparatively new form of tyranny), parents could "vote with their feet" by removing their children from any school that did not do the job. It was a good, sensible, fair system and it worked.

And don't think that poor families were left out in the cold. Even back then, there was also provision for them. For example, the Pennsylvania colony provided scholarships for poor students to attend private schools, in addition to the private philanthropy of individuals and businesses. This same tactic has been suggested in recent years as a means for families to escape bad schools by granting them, poor or not, tax credits or vouchers. These could be used at the parents' discretion to move their kids from failing schools to better ones. But predictably, such proposals have met with the stiffest resistance from the teachers' unions and many other liberal groups. A variety of excuses are given for this opposition, but it's always at bottom the same issue: government control. If competition were allowed in the school market as it normally exists in most markets, private schools would quickly put the government schools to shame and there would be a mass exodus from the government system. That would be disaster for the government elites who want to maintain control over the training of young citizens and for the educational unions who are about benefitting the employees rather than the students of the system.

It was not any real need that led to the creation of nonlocal, government-run education. It was agitation and lobbying by social engineers of the same stripe as the Unitarians and the Owenites. They were successful in getting government involved in education, gradually edging out most of the competition from private school. But they were not able to produce the crowning glory of government schooling: compulsory attendance.

The compulsion of attendance at school was finally accomplished with the help of big business interests. It wasn't easy to convince free Americans that citizens — of any age — could legally be incarcerated without having committed any crime. Public resistance was passionate and widespread. It took a long time to get the job done, but with the infusion of millions of dollars from men such as steel tycoon Andrew Carnegie and other industrialists, opposition was eventually overcome, in large part by the assurance that it was "for your own good." Sound familiar? Today we see a steady erosion of our freedom as government tightens its net of regulation in a hundred different arenas once considered "our own business," all in the name of "our own good." And government schooling has conditioned most of us to consent to being told what to do by elites, as if we weren't qualified to decide on our own as to what is "for our own good."

The motivation of the big business interests in education was similar to that of other social planners. American society had always been characterized by self-employment. In those days, you usually didn't chant the mantra of "getting a job." You thought in terms of staking your claim, starting your business, or opening your shop. This was a problem for the big-business guys. They didn't want a million young entrepreneurs starting businesses to compete with the ones they themselves had built. What's more, they needed a large population of consumers to buy their newly mass-produced products rather than doing for themselves. A mother who was competent at the spinning wheel was unlikely to be a regular customer for factory-produced cloth.

What the new millionaires wanted was an American who was content to work on an assembly line rather than starting his own business and valued the convenience of buying products more than the satisfaction of doing for himself. They had the savvy to watch the social engineers as they devised the means to collect and indoctrinate children to their way of thinking and figured the system could work for them, too. By the beginning of the 20th century, huge amounts of cash were finding their way into politicians' pet projects, endowments for teachers' colleges and other avenues through which the desires of big business could be reflected in the makeup of the schooling process. Finally, combining their money with the prestige of famous educational institutions and the influence of the publishing industry (popular newspapers, etc.), the industrialists saw a shared dream come true as compulsory attendance gradually became a fact of life in state after state. Over a hundred years ago, the control of child training came under the control of government and those who exerted their influence on it. Marx and Engels would be proud.

Ultimately, it is government that controls the public schools. They are just as much government training camps as any school in any Communist country. Government issues the mandates, swayed from year to year by the influence of teachers' unions and other big money interests. The atheist Owenites would be pleased with the Supreme Court's rulings of the 1960s that removed regular Bible reading and prayer from the classroom and with the constant attacks on free enterprise. The early Unitarians would be gratified that the concept of sin is never mentioned in class. Still, one suspects that both groups might have second thoughts if they could see the other effects of their dream of government control in education from today's vantage point. Our whole society has been dumbed down and stripped of its moral compass as schooling has ceased to be about the formation of character and thinking skills, and converted to the teaching of politically correct attitudes.

"Public" education will destroy America if it is not curbed. You've heard horror stories (at least if you've ever listened to talk radio) about just how bad the system is. I could go on and on just telling you what I know from my own experience and reading, but it would be better for you to read even one good book on the subject. You could try *Inside American Education* by Thomas Sowell or *Public Education Against America* by Marlin Maddoux. The very first book I'd recommend, though, is *Dumbing Us Down* by John Taylor Gatto, my very favorite education author. I have read it over and over again, and nearly torn it to pieces with my underlining pen. I recommend it to everybody. If you want a complete understanding of the process of how government got control of education, read his longer work *The Underground History of American Education.* A quick Internet search for articles by these or many other authors would be well worthwhile.

Speaking of Mr. Gatto, in *Dumbing Us Down* he lists seven lessons that children learn in public school. I'll list them below with a little explanatory material, but keep in mind that this is a man who attended public schools as a child and taught in them for 30 years. He was twice "Teacher of the Year" for the New York City public schools and once for the state of New York. When he says that these hidden lessons are the main curriculum of schooling, it would be wise to listen to him:

1. Confusion

Everything I teach is out of context. I teach the un-relating of everything. I teach dis-connections. I teach too much: the orbiting of planets, the law of large numbers, gymnasium, choral singing, assemblies, surprise guests, fire drills, computer languages, parents' nights . . . pull-out programs, guidance with strangers my students may never see again, standardized tests, age-segregation unlike anything seen in the outside world. . . . What do any of these things have to do with each other? . . . School sequences are crazy. There is no particular reason for any of them. . . . School subjects are learned . . . like children learn the catechism or memorize the Thirty-nine Articles of Anglicanism. . . . I teach the un-relating of everything, and infinite fragmentation the opposite of cohesion. . . . I teach you how to accept confusion as your destiny.

You can see how this lesson would be useful to tyrants. Confused people have a very hard time thinking for themselves. They tend to believe what they're told and do what they're told. People who aren't sure what they believe are unlikely to take a stand upon it.

2. Class Position

I teach that students must stay in the class where they belong. I don't know who decides my kids belong there but that's not my business. . . . Over the years the variety of ways children are numbered by schools has increased dramatically, until it is hard to see the human beings plainly under the weight of numbers they carry. . . . If I do my job well, the kids can't even imagine themselves somewhere else, because I've shown them how to envy and fear the better classes and how to have contempt for the dumb classes. . . . The lesson of numbered classes is that everyone has a proper place in the pyramid and there is no way out of your place. . . .

Here's a lesson in not aiming too high. Politicians, teachers, bureaucrats, and newscasters are all professionals. Don't try this at home.

3. Indifference

I teach children not to care too much about anything. . . . I do it by demanding that they become totally involved in my lessons, jumping up and down in their seats with anticipation, competing vigorously with each other for my favor. . . . But when the bell rings I insist they drop whatever it is we have been doing and proceed quickly to the next work station. They must turn on and off like a light switch. Nothing important is ever finished. . . . Indeed, the lesson of bells is that no work is worth finishing, so why care too deeply about anything? Years of bells will condition all but the strongest. . . .

I can vaguely remember the feeling he speaks of. I used to do what I had to do in order to keep the teacher off my back, but as soon as the bell rang I forgot about it and headed for the next class. I seem to remember that we never finished the textbook by the end of the year, which gave the impression of artificiality. If the last two chapters weren't necessary, why were the previous chapters? I can see how kids could get in the habit of not caring about their work and just putting in the time. I've seen that attitude in myself and definitely in most of the people who have worked for me over the years.

4. Emotional Dependency

By stars and red checks, smiles and frowns, prizes, honors, and disgraces, I teach kids to surrender their will to the predestinated chain of command. Rights may be granted or withheld by any authority without appeal, because rights do not exist inside a school . . . unless school authorities say they do. . . . Sometimes free will appears right in front of me in pockets of children angry, depressed, or happy about things outside my ken; rights in such matters cannot be recognized by schoolteachers, only privileges that can be withdrawn, hostages to good behavior.

One thing children do learn in school is the habit of doing what they're told. One thing that helps with this is requiring children to do things that make no sense, such as copying vocabulary words off the blackboard. A childhood full of such exercises is great training in doing what one is told without thinking whether the instructions make sense or whether the person giving orders has any right to do so.

5. Intellectual Dependency

Good students wait for a teacher to tell them what to do. It is the most important lesson, that we must wait for other people, better trained than ourselves, to make the meanings of our lives. The expert makes all the important choices; only I, the teacher, can determine what my kids must study, or rather, only the people who pay me can make those decisions, which I then enforce. If I'm told that evolution is a fact instead of a theory, I transmit that as ordered, punishing deviants who resist what I have been told to tell them to think. . . . Of the millions of things of value to study . . . what few we have time for . . . is decided by my faceless employers. . . . We've built a way of life that depends on people doing what they are told because they don't know how to tell themselves what to do. It's one of the biggest lessons I teach.

6. Provisional Self-Esteem

I teach that a kid's self-respect should depend on expert opinion. My kids are constantly evaluated and judged. A monthly report . . . is sent into a student's home to elicit approval or mark exactly, down to a single percentage point, how dissatisfied with the child a parent should be. . . . Although some people might be surprised how little time or reflection goes into making up these mathematical records, the cumulative weight of these objective-seeming documents establishes a profile that compels children to arrive at certain decisions about themselves and their futures based on the casual judgment of strangers. Self-evaluation, the staple of every major philosophical system . . . is never considered a factor. The lesson of report cards, grades, and tests is that children should not trust themselves or their parents but should instead rely on the evaluation-certified officials. People need to be told what they are worth.

7. One can't hide.

I teach students that they are always watched, that each is under constant surveillance by myself and my colleagues. There are no private spaces for children, there is no private time. . . . Students are encouraged to tattle on each other or even to tattle on their own parents. Of course, I encourage parents to file reports about their own child's wayward-ness too. . . . I assign a type of extended schooling called "homework," so that the effect of surveillance . . . travels into private households, where students might otherwise use free time to learn something unauthorized from a fa-ther or mother, by exploration, or by apprenticing to some wise person in the neighborhood. Disloyalty to the idea of schooling is a devil always ready to find work for idle hands. The meaning of constant surveillance and denial of privacy is that no one can be trusted, that privacy is not legitimate . . . children must be closely watched if you want to keep a society under tight central control. Children will follow a private drummer if you can't get them into a uniformed marching band.

That's the problem, that somebody, lots of somebodies in fact, want to keep our society under central control. That is the opposite of freedom and self-determination. It's also the opposite of personal responsibility.

To put in my own two cents' worth, though, don't even think that reforming the public schools is going to fix the problem. Reform movements have come and gone since at least the 1950s, and the situation is worse than ever. The system needs to come down. Education must be privatized. Compulsory attendance is wrongful incarceration of innocent citizens so it must be stopped. I'm not saying that we shouldn't fight to do everything possible to improve the schools. Most American children will be in those schools for at least the foreseeable future, so we need to do what we can to make their lives better. I'm just saying your long-term goal should be getting the government out of the upbringing of children. Until we break the government's illegitimate monopoly on education, private education won't be able to offer a better way to children. Many parents can't afford to pay taxes to support government schools as well as pay private school tuition. That is, unless they are willing and able to homeschool their children, and most people aren't. Yet.

So what are you going to do about it?

This is the society you've inherited and it is what it is. The masses are trained in government schools and taught to be passive. The elite are trained in private academies and Ivy League universities to be leaders. Your job is to defy the culture, swim against the current, and do your part in the fight to bring educational freedom back to America. But what can be done?

First, promote home education. Talk to your friends about it. Write letters to the editor about it, including documentation showing how well it works academically and socially. There's plenty of information on the Internet to use for ammunition. Remember, you're thinking in terms of leadership. Exhibit some yourself by asking your friends to write letters as well.

In 2007, the National Endowment for the Arts published a report entitled "Reading at Risk." The report was an alarming picture of reading ability across America. The National Endowment for the Arts is a liberal organization, and it's surprising to see them publish such an indictment as this. Not often does such a group, created by the federal government, call attention to a basic educational problem. Giving credit where credit is due, they have done all of us a service by making it the topic of a published report. The Endowment's chairman, Dana Gioia, stated, "This is a massive social problem. We are losing the majority of the new generation. They will not achieve anything close to their potential because of poor reading."

The report commented at length on the fact that fewer Americans are good readers and worse, fewer of them have the desire to read. It stated that nearly half of Americans in the age bracket of 18–24 never read books for pleasure. Why? No doubt the cheap and easy availability of electronic entertainment has something to do with it. But computer science has brought not only computer games and digitalized music to us, it has also brought easy access to zillions of books on e-readers and the computer screen. So the larger reason that people don't read is simply that it's hard for them to do so. Whereas nearly everybody could read well a hundred years ago, today we are a nation of semi-literates. Each generation that passes through our school system suffers more. According to the Endowment's paper, the number of 17 year olds who never read for pleasure was up from 9 percent in 1984 to 19 percent in 2004. It's not fun to read when it's a struggle to do so.

To quote the survey:

> Reading at Risk is not a report that the National Endowment for the Arts is happy to issue. This comprehensive survey of American literary reading presents a detailed but bleak

assessment of the decline of reading's role in the nation's culture. For the first time in modern history, less than half of the adult population now reads literature, and these trends reflect a larger decline in other sorts of reading. Anyone who loves literature or values the cultural, intellectual, and political importance of active and engaged literacy in American society will respond to this report with grave concern.

But how do we respond? Unfortunately, the report doesn't tell us who the bad guy is. But conservatives know, because of a number of great books on the subject, including the 1955 best seller by Rudolph Flesch, *Why Johnny Can't Read.* Flesch wrote:

> The teaching of reading — all over the United States, in all the schools, in all the textbooks — is totally wrong and flies in the face of all logic and common sense.[1]

Since Flesch's book, there have been a number of books on the same subject, including Samuel Blumenfeld's 1973 work *The New Illiterates.* Sam is another great education writer.

It's too bad the Endowment report didn't make the same charge. The problem is government schooling with its "look-say" or "sight word" reading programs. They don't make any sense. The correct way to teach reading is with a phonics method and lots of reading to children by adults.

So it is no secret that Americans are lousy readers. And sensible people know that this is a devastating problem. People who don't read well and widely are poorly informed people. And people who are not well informed are not well equipped for life. They are also poorly equipped to be citizens in a free country where their hope of remaining free depends on their ability to know what is going on in their society and take effective measures to keep things on the right track. We know that there is a big problem and we know what the cure is. But all this liberal, tax-supported endowment group can do is express their "grave concern." You have to wonder why they bothered with the report if they weren't going to suggest an effective solution. But it would put one government agency in a bad light if it attacked another government agency — the school system — for creating the "new illiterates."

And once the report was issued, it pretty much disappeared. I don't remember hearing about it through the national media, do you? I'm old enough to remember another such report (a quite extensive one) that was issued in 1983 when Reagan was president and Dr. William Bennett was Secretary of Education. It came from the National Commission on Excellence in Education in April 1983:

> The educational foundations of our society are presently being eroded by a rising tide of mediocrity that threatens our very future as a nation and as a people. . . . If an unfriendly foreign power had attempted to impose on America the mediocre educational performance that exists today, we might well have viewed it as an act of war. As it stands, we have allowed this to happen to ourselves.

Or more accurately, our educational leadership did it to the rest of us. But the nation didn't rise up in indignation and demand radical change in education in 1983. Just as it didn't in 2007 when the report of the National Endowment for the Arts came out. Both reports just disappeared from the radar of public consciousness. We as a people have been too conditioned to believe that the solution to national problems lies beyond the reach of average citizens and only big shots in government have any power. So we complain for a while and then let things slide.

And unfortunately it's true that the education bureaucracy is so firmly established that the problems are not readily solved. These people have a statist agenda, and the publication of these reports indicates that they are succeeding rather than failing. The decline of reading ability in the populace means progress for socialism. People who can't read or just don't read are easily influenced and led. And misled.

Federal funding and federal laws have made the school bureaucracy into a fortress. We have come to accept federal government control of schooling even though there was no federal Department of Education until after Jimmy Carter (a Socialist) was elected president in 1976. Carter created the new federal agency in fulfillment of a campaign promise in exchange for the support of the National Education Association, the American Federation of Teachers, and other teachers' unions. And how do those unions stand on the welfare of kids in school? AFT president Albert Shanker said in 1985, "When schoolchildren start paying union dues, that's when I'll start representing the interests of schoolchildren."[2] You see, the teachers' unions, like the government education bureaucracy, are not about kids, they're about money and power.

Although there was no federal Department of Education prior to 1976, the federal government has been gradually seizing power over children for a long time. For example, President Lyndon Johnson, a radical liberal Socialist, in 1965 signed into law the Elementary and Secondary Education Act. This law was reauthorized and its life extended another six years by President George Bush and renamed the No Child Left Behind Act. Too bad Bush didn't just let it die. And call for the abolition of the Department of Education altogether. Instead, he renamed the department's Washington headquarters the Lyndon B. Johnson

Building. Ironically, I recently stayed in a hotel across the street from that building.

Back to the Endowment report, which we could summarize in one sentence: "Americans in all groups are reading less than ever before and the decline is faster than ever before, especially among young people." Let me commend you once again for having gotten this far in this book.

How can this happen in a nation that spends more money on schooling than any nation ever has before? It was intended to happen. But Chairman Gioia wonders: "What is to be done? There is surely no single solution to the present dilemma, just as there is no single cause."[3] Stated that way, it's hard to argue with his logic. One could say that there are many problems, including uninvolved parents, school discipline, television, unqualified teachers, etc. But the simple fact is that when phonics instruction was the norm for public schooling, nearly everybody learned to read well. When, amid the national upheaval created by World War II in the 1940s, phonics was quietly replaced in the schools by "sight word" reading programs, Americans began to lose their literacy. It's interesting to note that the rate of literacy was significantly lower soon thereafter. For instance, recruits tested for military induction for the Korean War in the 1950s scored drastically lower on the reading portion of the exam than did their World War II counterparts only a few years before.

If Chairman Gioia really wants to know what needs to be done to fix American literacy, he should read books by Flesch, Blumenfeld, or a number of other writers to find out. The problem is that the educational "powers that be" don't really want it fixed. That would interfere with the advancement of their power. The problem is simple: deliberate educational malpractice by people in leadership.

What do those folks believe about reading? Here's a quote from three professors of the "sight word" or "whole language" approach in a book titled *Whole Language: What's the Difference?*

> From a whole-language perspective, reading (and language use in general) is a process of generating hypotheses in a meaning-making transaction in a sociohistorical context. As a transactional process . . . reading is not a matter of "getting the meaning" from the text, as if that meaning were in the text waiting to be decoded by the reader.
>
> Rather, reading is a matter of readers using the cues print provides and the knowledge they bring with them (of language subsystems, of the world) to construct a unique interpretation.
>
> Moreover, that interpretation is situated: readers' creations (not retrievals) of meaning with text vary, depending on their purposes of reading and the expectations of others in the reading event. This view of reading implies that there is no single "correct" meaning for a given text, only plausible meanings.[4]

Good grief. That bit of psychobabble sounds like something you'd hear in conversation at a pot party.

Let me see if I can get this straight. Reading is not a matter of "getting the meaning" from the text. It's a matter of "using the cues" to "construct a unique interpretation." I guess that means that it doesn't matter what the writer meant by his words, just what the reader decides that they mean.

And there's no single "correct" meaning for a text, "only plausible meanings." So I guess on my next Valentine's Day card I can write to my wife, "You're a homely hag," and she can read, "You're a vision of loveliness that makes my heart pound uncontrollably." Somehow I'm not sure she would be likely to construct that unique interpretation.

So the next time you're helping a child learn to read, tell him not to worry about what's written in the word, but what he thinks it means. After all, it's not a matter of "getting the meaning" but of creating the meaning. What gibberish.

I'm sure you can see by now that "education" as it has come to be understood today, is not about teaching children to be all they can be and preparing them to make their own way in life. Rather it is about training young people to move as a mass, to memorize rather than think critically, and depend on someone else to provide them with a living. This is the kind of person that fulfills the preferences of social engineers, big business, and aspiring tyrants in government.

It is also a cash cow. It provides opportunity for educational unions, who work for their members' (teachers and administrators) welfare rather than that of students, and for a wide array of other employees, contractors, and suppliers. Long is the roster of those who make millions supplying books, desks, soap, soda straws, globes, and construction services. It is a huge industry that has attracted flocks of speculators, many of whom have an intense interest in keeping the system as it is. That's why reform movements have come and gone for over half a century without improving schooling much. It's not there for the benefit of the children.

So to understand the cultural warfare going on in the arena of primary and secondary education (elementary through high school), we have to see it in terms of working within the system at the same time as we strive to break the illegitimate monopoly of the government. We need to look for ways to minister to the students

— and the staff — who are in the system now and will be for the near future. At the same time, some of us must be working to repeal compulsory attendance laws, promote alternative forms of schooling, and push initiatives such as tuition tax credits to give poor and middle-class families the option to leave failing government schools and seek education elsewhere.

To be fair, there are some other remedies being pursued these days such as minimum standards, national testing, a national curriculum, merit pay for teachers, etc. I don't have a lot of faith in those ideas myself, because it leaves so much power in the hands of bureaucrats rather than communities. Merit pay, for instance, sounds good in theory (better teachers get paid more), but who decides which teachers deserve it? You can bet it won't be decided by the students or their parents. And that is the only way to make education respond to the natural forces of the free market.

But we've only discussed half the battlefield of education. The policies that dictate daily life in most elementary and secondary schools issue from government departments and the university community. Both of these institutions are in turn influenced by the pressure brought on them by various interest groups. These groups often operate under the radar, but their tentacles have a strong grip nevertheless. An example would be the pharmaceutical companies. These people make their money in a perfectly legitimate and valuable way: they develop and sell drugs that we all depend on to improve and extend our lives. But what is far less evident is the effect they have on all of us through their giving practices. Large financial endowments from drug companies have long been a power in the practice of medicine. Why? Because medical schools are like anybody else. They don't want to bite the hand that feeds them because they know the food supply will dry up. As a result, the practice of American medicine is heavy on the use of drugs. It is also much more about treating disease than preventing it. In some countries, much of the attention given to health is in the form of prevention and much of the treatment is based on natural rather than pharmaceutical.

My chiropractor once told me that some physicians — I think he meant most physicians — get through their training without ever having taken a course in nutrition. That sounded impossible in view of the importance of nutrition to health. How could they train a health professional without making him an expert in nutrition? But when I asked our family doctor about it, he confirmed it. He said what little nutrition he had been taught in medical school was mixed in with something else. There had been little attention paid to it and no courses that were totally dedicated to it. I wondered how this could be possible. Veterinarians spend huge amounts of time studying the nutritional needs of dogs, cats, and horses. Why would doctors not get at least as much training in human nutrition?

The answer comes, as it so often does, when we follow the money trail. A medical school that taught students about keeping people from becoming sick would produce doctors who didn't need to dispense as many drugs. Drug companies would not be racing to dump millions on a school like that. And that is one of many examples of how money from outside the education system influences education and its effects on the citizenry, every day of our lives.

Other groups are less about money than philosophy. The best example of this is the Communist Party. You seldom hear the word Communist since the fall of the Berlin Wall in the 1980s and the collapse of the Soviet Union shortly after. But the Communist philosophy is alive and well. The continents of Africa and South America are largely dominated by Communist, or to use the more generic word, Socialist governments. In our country, communism has gone out of style and so operates much more underground than openly. But it is still pervasively influential in liberal political circles and on our university campuses.

I was in high school during the hottest years of the Vietnam War. To you it is just a chapter in the history books, but to me it was a defining characteristic of the youth culture in which I lived and moved. It was the springtime of free love (meaning promiscuous immorality), recreational drugs, widespread teen rebellion, and hard rock music. Young people who had been respectful and clean-cut at home went to college and learned to despise authority, hate their country, shed their religious disciplines, and throw away their morals. Opposition to America's involvement in Vietnam provided a common cause and an assumed element of justification for idealistic young people who wanted something important to believe in while yet dispensing with their families' traditional values.

The growth of Communist philosophy was both a cause and a result of this strange era in our history. A Communist group calling itself Students for a Democratic Society (SDS; which was the opposite of the fact) arose from some shadowy hinterland and took root in the fertile soil of the youth culture. The root system spread like wire grass and shoots popped up at college after college. SDS operatives organized war protests on and off campus, and shaggy-haired kids burned draft cards, smoked dope, played loud music, and screamed slogans. "H__ no, we won't go!" became the watchword. Students disrupted classes, damaged school property, and occupied administrative offices. The war was the issue they used to justify their belligerence, but the movement was more generally a rebellion against authority, godly moral standards, and traditional values and responsibility.

The Communist honchos of the SDS must have been laughing their heads off in private as they watched a whole generation of young Americans swing radically away from their worthy cultural moorings. It was all part of a process known as destabilization. They wanted to destabilize the anchors of our society: religion, family loyalty, morals, respect for law, patriotism. They knew something I learned in my first high school debate class: to convince people to make a major change, you must convince them there is something seriously wrong with the status quo. You must present a need, or needs, and persuade people that they are real and serious. That's what the SDS and other Socialist groups did with the Vietnam issue. They were also smart enough to know that they needed for young people en masse to reject their culture's traditional values before they could get them to follow a different drummer. They had learned it from their heroes, Karl Marx and Friedrich Engels. Remember it was Engels who had taught them to "separate a people from their roots" in order to change a free society to a communistic one. So the Communist subversives took advantage of youthful idealism, surging hormones, the new-found personal freedom of the campus, and a hot-button current issue to capture a generation.

In the 40 years since I first encountered the college scene, much has changed and much has remained the same. Some of those long-haired kids in their tie-dyed shirts, ripped jeans, love beads, and sandals have merged back into more traditional ways. But a big segment of the gang never got away from college. They're professors and deans now, and they're still carrying the Socialist standard. It's been said that communism is about dead everywhere except on

American college faculties. That numerical minority would be comforting, were it not for the knowledge that those colleges and universities are supplying the leadership for the education system that is training 90 percent of our young people.

At this point, let me say plainly what I've been trying to illustrate in this chapter so far. My premise is this: The education system all around you in America today is not about educating young people. It is about controlling them. It's being accomplished in several devious ways.

One of those ways is the deliberate dumbing down of our national literacy. When the decision was made somewhere in high places to replace the time-tested phonetic method of reading (letters stand for sounds) with the "look-say" method (letters stand for ideas), we saw our nation go from being a nation that could read well and liked to, to a nation full of functional illiterates. We have a hard time reading, so we don't enjoy it and don't do it much. You used to hear about a "well-read" person. They are rare anymore. That means we don't wrestle with ideas as much as we used to, preferring instead to listen to talking heads on TV that tell us what to think. Of course the widespread availability of electronic news and entertainment has in recent times increased the tendency of Americans not to read. Watching and listening is a lot less mental work. But people who read less think less. And people who don't think are easy to brainwash.

We've also structured our schools in a way that discourages real learning. Mr. Gatto's seven lessons of confusion, class position, indifference, emotional dependency, intellectual dependency, provisional self-esteem, and constant surveillance have been built into the system of our schools. Long ago, schools required students to research, reason, record, and relate knowledge to real life. Now students spend their time memorizing information that has been spoon-fed to them through books and lectures and forget most of it as soon as the test is over. Critical thinking is not taught. By dividing children by age instead of readiness level, many kids are studying material that is either above or below their ability to advance, while the age segregation keeps them from developing the traditional loyalties to parents and siblings. Researching and reasoning skills have been replaced with memorization, short-answer test questions, and true-false guesswork. Pointless busywork, homework, and a kaleidoscope of extracurricular activities gobble up time that could otherwise be spent exploring the world of family and community. The peer group, with its absence of the wisdom produced only by long life experience, socializes children to delay growing up far beyond natural seasons.

Anti-family, anti-morality, anti-biblical philosophies have permeated schools down to the earliest grades, having come in through the college community of the 1960s and 1970s along with the textbook publishing industry. Schools and texts that once taught solid academic content along with reverence, responsibility, discipline, and patriotism have nearly vanished from the land. In their place are schools administered and taught by the young Socialist radicals of the sixties and even their protégés from their early days of teaching. Text materials have been dumbed down with important information such as our founding principles left out, and nontraditional texts such as *Heather Has Two Mommies* and *King and King* are teaching values that few parents want their children to learn. In fact, as I write this it is recent news that California has just passed a law requiring the teaching of "gay" history in the public schools.

School leadership is still being drawn from a collegiate community that overwhelmingly rejects traditional, biblical American values. Education majors are the lowest-scoring group as compared with majors in all other academic disciplines,[5] and much of their study time is taken up with "pedagogy" courses that have little to do with real teaching and learning. Teacher certification has been statistically proven to be irrelevant to success in teaching, yet is still required to get a job teaching in the government school system.[6] Were they still alive, Ronald Reagan couldn't teach government in the public schools, Einstein couldn't teach science, and Mozart couldn't teach music. No "education" courses, no credential.

So what is the army of God to do about this nationwide mess? Is it too deeply entrenched to hope for the radical change that is needed to reverse the process? No. Not if you believe in the God that I know.

First, we pray. That's always the first and most important thing we do. Without the blessing of God, we'd be toast even if worldly conditions were hunky-dory. With it, we can overcome any obstacle. The schemes of evil men are nothing to God. Spiritual weapons first.

Then we must use every material weapon we have. For our own families, we must first protect ourselves and our children. Personally, I would never even consider sending my child to a government school, even the so-called good ones. There are no good ones, if only because there are none where the Bible is the most respected textbook. If you're a student in a government school now, appeal to your parents to get you out and teach you at home, or help you teach yourself. Tons of great Americans have done just that. If that option doesn't work for your family, a little research will reveal several good opportunities to attend a Christian school through scholarships, work-sudy programs, and the like. If you can't get out of school, watch for the things I've been talking about in this chapter. Read books and articles from long-ago times when

Americans were still being properly educated. Read modern conservative writers and note where they agree with each other and where they disagree. Practice looking at different sides of issues and resisting the "easy way" of believing the first opinion you read. Determine that you will form your own opinions after having looked at different sources, and refuse to make up your mind about an issue when you're not yet satisfied you have enough data and have thought it over enough. Remember, it's no sin to *not* have an opinion on every issue you hear about. It's far better than coming to a hasty or ill-informed opinion. Learn to live with the discomfort of not yet being able to take a stand. It's perhaps as important as being willing to take an unpopular stand. So take responsibility for your own education.

Some of you need to start private schools. These can be non-profit, like our church's Christian school. Or, you can start a proprietary school like the prep schools, where families pay for their children's education through tuition and the school is not tax-exempt but hopefully makes a profit. That's how most of the wealthy elite families do it.

We also need more people encouraging homeschooling. Somebody with financial resources should advertise in all the major newspapers that homeschooling is legal, feasible, and successful. A lot of people need to be in business meeting the needs of homeschooling families by teaching them how to do it and supplying materials. That's how I make my living, as do many people I know. But there's room for many more. The movement is going to keep growing, with new families starting up every year. Also, we need more people fighting to keep our legal freedom to homeschool. The statists and God-haters detest Christian home education and are ceaselessly working to attack it through education laws, child abuse charges, and a number of other methods. So we need lawyers and activists.

With politics so deeply embedded in the education problem, we need people fighting there, too. Lawmakers need to be lobbied so that the interest of freedom in education is represented. We need to end the locking up of children through compulsory attendance laws. Some people will object that some parents won't care if their children learn or not, and won't bother to send them to any school if the law doesn't require it. My answer to that is history. There have always been a few parents — a very few — who haven't bothered to see that their children are educated. But education overall was far better in America before compulsory attendance than after. And basing a policy for all on the needs of a tiny minority is foolish, especially when it infringes on personal freedom and family sovereignty. Even with the present laws, plenty of children skip school regularly. But natural curiosity and enlightened self-interest have always motivated learning far better than compulsion. Remember, it's compulsory attendance, not compulsory education. You're permitted to leave school at 18, regardless of whether you've learned anything or not. They just want to keep you institutionalized for the prescribed number of years. We also must fight for the improvement of curriculum in the public schools through weeding out texts that are weak on content or teach junk like "tolerance" and values clarification. We need to agitate for a return to solid academic knowledge and the expulsion of silly, half-baked theories. We need to push for reform that includes age integration and critical thinking skills. We need to demand the teaching of traditional values and absolutes of morality.

But all these things will be very tough to move forward because the powers in education are so deeply entrenched and supported by powerful political and financial interests. Most of all, we need educational freedom so that there will be many kinds of schools and other training (apprenticeships and internships, for example). Anybody who wants to teach should be free to do so, with the student or his family deciding whom to be taught by, and voting with their feet if they are unsatisfied with the education they get for their money. Tuition tax credits would be a great step in that direction. Eventually we want to rid ourselves entirely of taxes that support education of course, but tuition tax credits would be a hugely helpful and much more feasible intermediate step. When we get that done, many new schools will arise and provide superior alternatives for the spending of our educational dollars. Then public schools will have to change or collapse for lack of students.

We need Christians to teach. We need them to teach their own children at home, to teach in Christian schools, and to teach in public schools. I would never send a Christian kid to public school as a "missionary," but I heartily encourage Christian teachers to capitalize on the relationships they can have with kids, mostly from non-Christian homes, to influence them for the gospel.

Some of us need to write books and articles about education, showing the public that there are other ways to get an education than submitting to the dictates of government and swallowing all their propaganda. Americans are already tired of their children not being educated, and we need to encourage that discontent. If we can show the citizenry how they're being ripped off — which most of them only vaguely understand — we might just start a Tea Party in the realm of education.

Endnotes

1. Rudolf Flesch, *Why Johnny Can't Read — and What You Can Do about It* (New York: Harper, 1955).

2. Congressional Record, Aug. 1985.

3. http://thenewamerican.com/opinion/sam-blumenfeld/6877-national-endow-ment-for-the-arts-sounds-alarm-on-literacy.

4. Carole Edelsky, Bess Altwerger, and Barbara Flores, *Whole Language: What's the Difference?* (Portsmouth, NH: Heinemann, 1991), p. 19.

5. http://jte.sagepub.com/content/40/4/49.abstract.

6. See Jay P. Greene, *Education Myths: What Special Interest Groups Want You to Believe About Our Schools — and Why It Isn't So* (Lanham, MD: Rowman & Littlefield, 2005), p. 59–70.

Chapter 7

THE MEDIA

In the winter of early 1968 I was a high school sophomore whose favorite subject in school was wrestling practice. My interests were pretty local so I wasn't up on current events and national news. But nobody could ignore the news reports that came blasting across the evening airwaves on the last day of January 1968. It was all about the Tet Offensive.

The Vietnam War had been raging for several years, but President Johnson and General Westmoreland, the top military dog over there, assured us that it was slowly winding down. There was light at the end of the tunnel because the Communist North Vietnamese and the guerrilla Viet Cong had suffered such great losses that they were no longer capable of mounting a large-scale offensive. America and her little friend South Vietnam were winning.

Then came Tet — the Vietnamese New Year. Both sides had proclaimed a two-day cease-fire, but Communist governments are not known for keeping promises. Some 80,000 Communist troops attacked over a hundred South Vietnamese towns and cities, along with many American military bases in the country. It was the biggest offensive yet launched by either side during the entire war.

For the most part, the attack was an utter failure. The North Vietnamese and Viet Cong forces were decimated, suffering crippling losses in men and material. Their advance was stopped in its tracks by superior American training, equipment, and firepower. During the Tet season and the months following, over 45,000 Communist troops were killed. The effort had been a massive defeat for the Communist North and a resounding victory for the South Vietnamese and their American allies.

Then somehow the tables got turned. But it didn't happen on the battlefield. It was the American news media that did it, and they might fairly be given the credit for America's withdrawal from the country and the fact that the people of South Vietnam now live in slavery to communism.

After the conclusion of the first phase of the offensive, Hanoi (the North Vietnamese capital) realized that its sacrifices might not have been in vain. General Tran Do, North Vietnamese commander at the battle of Hue, gave some insight into how defeat was translated into victory:

> In all honesty, we didn't achieve our main objective, which was to spur uprisings throughout the South. Still, we inflicted heavy casualties on the Americans and their puppets, and this was a big gain for us. As for making an impact in the United States, it had not been our intention — but it turned out to be a fortunate result.[1]

He was referring to the help that the Communist cause received from the likes of Walter Cronkite, "the most trusted man in America."

Cronkite was only one of many news icons who declared the war to be unwinnable as a result of the Tet Offensive. But he carried more weight than most, perhaps more than any other reporter. He was known as "America's anchor man," and when he died in 2009 at the age of 92 he was lionized in eulogies all over the country.

Cronkite's mellow, fatherly voice was familiar to most Americans, even to 15-year-old me. While I viewed the evening news mostly as a chronological barrier between me and the more interesting prime time programming, nearly everybody watched it. Cronkite emotionally reported to us the assassinations of President John Kennedy and Martin Luther King. He was exuberant when he told us on Sunday, July 20, 1969, that a man had walked on the moon. He was a part of life if you grew up in those days. He was among the pioneers of television news.

When Cronkite made a trip to Vietnam to see for himself what was going on, he returned to tell the country that the best America could hope for in that war-torn country was a negotiated cease-fire. Up until then, the majority of Americans believed that our military could roll right over small and ill-eqipped North Vietnam, even with the assistance they received from Communist China and the USSR. But news reports affect public opinion, and Cronkite's word carried extra weight.

One of President Johnson's aides, Bill Moyers, watched the Cronkite report with the president. "The president flipped off the set," Mr. Moyers recalled, "and said, 'If I've lost Cronkite, I've lost middle America.' "[2] That's the power of the media.

When we talk about the media, we usually mean the media (plural of "medium") by which we receive news. That includes the "mainstream media," a term we conservatives normally use to describe the primarily liberal television, radio, newspapers, and magazines. By the 1980s and 1990s the mainstream news media had become so slanted toward a leftist (statist) philosophy that a good-sized percentage of the population was becoming unsatisfied, but there wasn't much of an alternative source for news. Around 1990 two developments broke the statist stranglehold on the delivery of news. These were the twin tidal waves of talk radio and the Internet.

Neither talk radio nor the Internet was new. But they swarmed into public consciousness in the late 80s and early 90s, becoming venues for the spreading of information that could finally compete with the big news conglomerates. As the science of blogging developed, it was discovered that anybody with a computer and an Internet connection could shoot out his own ideas just as rapidly as the traditional media. Almost overnight, everybody was "online." At the same time, Rush Limbaugh was revolutionizing radio talk broadcasting with his three-hour, Monday-through-Friday show. Limbaugh's mix of insightful conservative opinion and cheerfully sarcastic humor won him millions of fans and a number of competitors. New nationally syndicated talk shows appeared, most of them broadcasting news and commentary from a decidedly libertarian and conservative viewpoint. At last there was a powerful balancing factor to the steadily liberal reporting of news.

And it was needed. Surveys show that people who work in mainstream media are far more likely to be liberal in philosophy than the general public in the United States. The Rothman-Lichter studies also showed that they are motivated to influence their readers and listeners toward their leftist values. It's usually obvious in what they choose to report or ignore, as well as how they report it.

One of the most interesting instances of propaganda in media is a campaign ad that was shown on television during the presidential campaign of 1964 between Lyndon Johnson and Barry Goldwater. Goldwater had mentioned the possibility of using nuclear weapons to end the war in Vietnam. Johnson immediately seized upon the public's fear of the gargantuan power of nuclear weaponry and created what became known as the "Daisy ad." Here is Wikipedia's description of the ad:

> "Daisy," sometimes known as "Daisy Girl" or "Peace, Little Girl," was a controversial campaign television advertisement. Though aired only once (by the campaign), during a September 7, 1964, telecast . . . it was a factor in President Lyndon B. Johnosn's landslide victory over Barry Goldwater in the 1964 presidential election and an important turning point in political and advertising history. Its creator was Tony Schwartz of Doyle Dane Bernbach, the advertising agency that was handling the account for the presidential campaign of Johnson. It remains one of the most controversial political advertisements ever made.
>
> The advertisement begins with a little girl (four-year-old Monique M. Corzilius) standing in a meadow with chirping birds, picking the petals of what appears to be a daisy flower while counting each petal slowly. Because little Monique does not know her numbers perfectly, she repeats some and says others in the wrong order, all of which adds to her childlike appeal. When she reaches "nine," an ominous-sounding male voice is then heard counting down a missile launch, and as the girl's eyes turn toward something she sees in the sky, the camera zooms in until her pupil fills the screen, blacking it out. When the countdown reaches zero, the blackness is replaced by the flash and mushroom cloud from a nuclear explosion.

As the firestorm rages, a voiceover from Johnson states, "These are the stakes! To make a world in which all of God's children can live, or to go into the dark. We must either love each other, or we must die." Another voiceover (sportscaster Chris Schenkel) then says, "Vote for President Johnson on November 3. The stakes are too high for you to stay home."

The attack ad was designed to capitalize on comments made by Republican presidential candidate Barry Goldwater about the possibility of using nuclear weapons in Vietnam.

As soon as the ad aired, Johnson's campaign was widely criticized for using the prospect of nuclear war, as well as the implication that Goldwater would start one, to frighten voters. The ad was immediately pulled, but the point was made, appearing on the nightly news and on conversation programs in its entirety. Jack Valenti, who served as a special assistant to Johnson, later suggested that pulling the ad was a calculated move, arguing that "it showed a certain gallantry on the part of the Johnson campaign to withdraw the commercial." Johnson's line "We must either love each other, or we must die" echoes W.H. Auden's poem "September 1, 1939" in which line 88 reads, "We must love one another or die." The words "children" and "the dark" also occur in Auden's poem.

In 1984, Walter Mondale's unsuccessful presidential campaign used ads with a similar theme to the Daisy ad. Mondale's advertisements cut between footage of children and footage of ballistic missiles and nuclear explosions, over a soundtrack of the song "Teach Your Children" by Crosby, Stills, Nash & Young.[3]

Now, keep in mind that this is an example of paid political advertising. It wasn't necessarily the opinion of the network that broadcast the commercial. But it is a good example of how the media can be used to powerfully get a point across through clever suggestive tactics. This sort of thing is used in news reporting all the time when the reporter or the network he works for has an agenda they want to accomplish, as in the case of Cronkite's opposition to the Vietnam War.

The Daisy ad made a deep impression on the American public partly because the liberal media had already been laying the groundwork. Though it was not nearly as established then as it is now, liberalism in news reporting had already laid the foundation that conservative ideas were not just obsolete but downright dangerous. And even though the ad was only run once because of the public outcry over its extremism, the Johnson campaign could rest assured that the news programs would replay it with comment over and over, so that it would get tons of free exposure. And they only had to pay for it once. Very clever.

The manipulation of news reporting is not surprising. Some of it occurs because reporters, editors, and bureau chiefs espouse liberal views themselves. Ultimately, though, the results come through top-down policies dictated by huge corporations who own one or more news agencies. An example would be CNN, the first 24-hour dedicated cable news channel, which is owned by media billionaire Ted Turner. Turner's liberal philosophy is well known. He donated a billion (yes, I said B–B–Billion) dollars to causes espoused by the United Nations and created the United Nations Foundation to broaden support for the UN. If you're not aware of it, the UN routinely does all it can to damage America.

Turner's own words clearly identify his philosophy. His many controversial statements earned him such nicknames as "The Mouth of the South" and "Captain Outrageous." Turner once called observers of Ash Wednesday "Jesus Freaks" and referred to opponents of abortion as "bozos." In 2008 Turner also commented on PBS's Charlie Rose television program that if global warming is not corrected, within ten years "most of the people will have died and the rest of us will be cannibals." Turner also said in the interview that he thought the United States should make drastic reductions in the nation's military budget and that Americans should have no more than two children. He also said that men should be prohibited from holding public office. "Men should be barred from public office for 100 years in every part of the world. . . . The men have had millions of years where we've been running things. We've screwed it up hopelessly. Let's give it to the women."[4]

In 1990 he created the Turner Foundation, which focuses on philanthropic grants in environment and population. That was the same year in which he created the environmental-themed cartoon series *Captain Planet and the Planeteers.*

In 1991 Turner became the first media figure to be named *Time* magazine's Man of the Year. *Time* is recognized as one of the most liberal, statist magazines in the country. A proponent of President Obama's healthcare bill, Turner has said, "We're the only first world country that doesn't have universal healthcare and it's a disgrace."[5] Not surprisingly, CNN is noted for a deep and consistent liberal bias in its programming, especially in its reporting of news.

The manipulation of news reporting is nothing new. In the *Congressional Record* of February 9, 1917, page 2947, Congressman Oscar Callaway of Texas made this statement:

> In March 1915, the J.P. Morgan interests, the steel, shipbuilding, and powder interest, and their subsidiary organizations got together 12 men high up in the newspaper world

and employed them to select the most influential newspapers in the United States and sufficient number of them to control generally the policy of the daily press. . . . They found it was only necessary to purchase the control of 25 of the greatest papers. An agreement was reached; the policy of the papers was bought, to be paid for by the month; an editor was furnished for each paper to properly supervise and edit information regarding the questions of preparedness, militarism, financial policies, and other things of national and international nature considered vital to the interests of the purchasers.

I have not been able to verify whether Congressman Callaway was correct in this statement, though I have seen it quoted in several sources. It's not hard to believe, though, considering the period of history in which it was made. At the time, England, Germany, and several other European countries were embroiled in World War I. In the United States, there was something going on called the preparedness movement. This group said that even though the United States had no immediate vital interest in the war, we should be building up our military forces in case we were drawn into it later. Callaway's opinion, which is pretty believable, was that powerful business interests wanted America to enter the war because it would create big new demand for their products and services.

In fact, by the time America entered the war in 1917, things had pretty much ground to a halt as the Allies and Germans found themselves in a virtual stalemate, their resources seriously depleted after three years of war. There are those historians today who believe that the war would have fizzled out had not America jumped in, helping England and France conquer Germany and impose upon her the harsh conditions of the Treaty of Versailles (including the repayment of the Allies' war debts by now-starving Germany). Those conditions were largely responsible for the financial devastation of Germany in the 1920s and helped pave the way for a desperate nation to turn to the fanatical Hitler, who promised restored prosperity and German supremacy in Europe.

Besides the ownership and management of news agencies, responsibility for the message of the media is shared by those who work in the trenches. Schools of journalism around the country supply the industry with a fresh supply of statist-minded candidates for reporters, editors, and bureau chiefs each year. These young people are light on critical thinking skills, and their supply of hard academic knowledge is scanty compared to those who major in more substantial courses of study. In fact, journalism as a major competes with education for a place as the least-respected field of academic pursuit. But these graduates are thoroughly grounded in liberal prejudice. Their selection and reporting of news items predictably represents that.

Have you ever noticed the use of the word "extreme" as it's applied to political beliefs in the reporting of news? It's often applied to conservative ideas and people, but never to liberal ideas or people. You'll read or hear about "extreme conservative" views, but never "extreme liberal" views. The suggestion is that liberals can never be extreme, weird, or outside the mainstream of thought. Liberals are always normal. Only conservatives can be extreme. They're dangerous people. A serious Christian is a Fundamentalist or "born again" as if it's some kind of a weird cult. But if there's a story about some Asian religious fanatic who blows up a bunch of innocent people, he's a Fundamentalist, too. Fundamentalist and fanatic have come to be regarded as synonyms.

Okay, we understand that the mainstream TV news, radio news, magazines, and newspapers are dominated by liberal, anti-biblical thought. What can we do? How can we compete with the power and reach of the *New York Times* or the *Washington Compost* — er, I mean, *Post*?

There are basically two avenues to do this. The first is to work through existing publications. The other is to establish new publications ourselves. To do the second, you can make several million dollars and buy a newspaper, television, or radio station. Or you can call in to talk radio, which a lot of people do. If you can afford it, you can advertise in existing media. One of the cheap and easy ways to use existing media is the time-honored practice of writing letters to the editor.

Do letters to the editor really have the potential to affect public opinion? You better believe it.

In our day, the Internet is giving the print media fits. Even the most popular newspapers, the ones with millions of copies circulating daily, are suffering from the competition of blogs, ezines, news websites, Youtube, and Facebook. These and other online means of communication are offering the public loads of information, sometimes even faster than the papers can. And they are mostly free or cheap. For that reason, newspapers are more interested than ever before in receiving letters to the editor on topics of interest to their readers. They want to keep the readers happy and they figure if you're interested in the topic you're writing about, other readers are, too. That doesn't mean at all that you should only submit letters to papers you subscribe to; it's just an indication of public interest.

Your letter has an impact on politics in more ways than one. First, it shares your opinion — hopefully, along with some convincing logic and evidence — with the many people who read the paper. So you have an effect on people who will vote, campaign for candidates, and work to influence legislators. Another important thing to remember is that politicians read the newspapers, too. It's a great way for them to keep a finger on the pulse of public opinion. And most politicians live and die for public opinion. If they see letters to the editor consistently taking one side of an issue, they are very likely to bear that in mind when they have an opportunity to influence that issue.

There has been plenty of media research done because newspapers need to know what the public wants, as any successful business must. And the research is clear that the Letters to the Editor section is one of the most often read parts of the paper.

I called the editor of our local paper and did a little research of my own. He told me that indeed, his paper also finds that the "Letters" section is very popular. In fact, he said it was perhaps the most-read section of the paper, with the possible exception of the obituaries. (I guess it makes sense; if I ever read the obits and found out I'm dead, I certainly wouldn't bother reading the editorial page.) He then told me how many copies of the paper they sell on an average day, how many people read each copy on average (two to three), what percentage read the editorial page, and based on that, we calculated an estimate of how many people read the letters to the editor each day. The conclusion? In our metropolitan area, which is about 75,000 in population, about 30,000 to 40,000 people read the letters to the editor on an average day. Wow.

This is one of the reasons your mom used to harp so much about spelling, punctuation, and grammar. Poorly written letters aren't likely to get printed in the paper (doesn't make the paper look good), and if they are, they're not going to be a good testimonial to the writer's cause.

Obviously, all this means that if you write a convincing letter you can sway a lot of opinions. Don't think, *But will people change their minds on an issue just reading a letter in the newspaper? I wouldn't.* You need to keep several things in mind. First of all, not everybody is as firm in his convictions as you are. Many people are more easily persuaded. Besides, there will be a lot of people reading your letter who don't have a strong opinion on the topic — they may never have thought about it until they see what you wrote. It may be a subject that they're not even aware of. Finally, don't forget the "bandwagon" effect. There are a certain number of people in any population who don't think for themselves and are most comfortable going along with the crowd, getting on the bandwagon. Your letter might be the one that tips the numerical scales in favor of your position on the issue. Rare indeed is the person who will quickly form an opinion that's contrary to the overwhelming majority, so write about what you're passionate about and ask others to do the same.

One more thing to remember: Your letters to the editor will have an impact on *what the newspaper itself decides to write about.* For instance, let's say you notice a tiny article in the "local" section of the paper about a proposed zoning change in your city. Ho hum, you say. Who cares about zoning? It's not in my neighborhood anyway.

But then you notice in the article that somebody has requested the zoning change in a certain part of town in order to allow him to put a topless bar there. Whoa. Different picture. So you write a very opinionated letter to the editor and get several people from your church to do the same. Not all of them will get published, but some probably will. When the editor, insightful fellow that he is, sees how much community interest there is in this issue, his eyebrows rise. Hmmm. There may be more of a story here than we thought. Instantly he dispatches cub reporter Jimmy Olson to the scene and he interviews the guy who wants to build the bar. Jimmy also calls the pastors of the two or three largest churches in town (at least the ones with a history of commenting on moral issues) and gets their input. They hadn't seen the two paragraphs the paper originally wrote on the subject, but now they're aware of it and they start to squawk. The liberals in the community hear about it and they take the opposing side. They write to the paper, whining about "freedom of expression," and now the issue is front-page stuff. Newspapers love controversy, because they know people don't buy papers to read about stuff everybody agrees on. You've just turned a two-paragraph article about zoning into a serious community issue. The paper will very likely put a more in-depth story in the next issue, perhaps even on the front page. Maybe they'll even run an editorial from the Great Man (editor) himself. You have influenced the newspaper's choice of topics and in the process brought the attention of the public to an important moral issue.

Time to get political. You call up the members of the city council and ask them why they would even consider putting such an establishment in an otherwise unsullied neighborhood of your fair city. Have your friends call as well, always well prepared to present their case. Do we really want influences like this here? Don't we have enough divorce, family breakdown, rape, other sexual assaults, and assorted violent crime in our hometown? A brief Internet search might yield some juicy statistics on crime in areas close to topless bars, giving you more ammunition for your city leaders and additional letters to the editor as well.

Go further and call the city prosecutor's office. He might be called the city attorney, attorney general, or something else. Ask him if topless bars are in fact legal in your city. If he cares anything about moral questions and takes his job seriously (and in many cases he will — often his job is an *elected* position) it may be that you can get him to investigate. Just maybe the guy who requested the zoning variance owns other establishments like the one he's proposing, and maybe one or more of them is in violation of some law. People like that usually aren't terribly scrupulous about complying with the law. They may be guilty of some violation of regulations regarding their liquor license, closing times, admission of minors, even tax evasion. If the prosecutor's office knows the public is concerned about this situation, they are more likely to take an interest as well. It wouldn't be good for their job security if they missed a violation that later came to light because a concerned citizen noticed something going on.

You could also call your elected representatives at the state level. It may very well be that there is a state law relating to this subject. By the way, these people listen to their constituents. They know who put them in office. If they hear from you often, they will remember your name. So write to them, call them, and go see them at their public appearances in your area. And campaign for the worthy ones. They will remember and listen when you speak.

With all that said, here are some guidelines for putting together an effective letter to the editor:

- **Pick a publication.** I've been writing about letters to local newspapers, but many different kinds of magazines and other publications entertain letters from readers. Write to a publication you enjoy reading. You may get an opinion before readers who had never thought about the subject before. Larger publications will get your opinion before more people, but smaller ones receive fewer letters and so will give you a better chance of getting your letter printed.

- **Pick a topic.** Write about something that excites your passions. You will be more likely to see your letter in print if your topic is also one that has been reflected in an article or letter in the same paper recently. If that's the case, respond with your own letter right away or your topic may be old news. This tactic will make your letter seem more relevant and help the editor quickly check the original article to verify your facts. Remember, editors are like anybody else in that they like people who make their lives easier. Don't write about your pet peeves. You'll be less likely to get published, and if you make a habit of this, other readers will eventually associate your name with a "ho-hum" feeling and tend to skip reading your future letters and stop taking you seriously as a commentator. You want to write about things that other people will find interesting, even if they had never thought about them before.

- **Get to the point**. State your issue up front both to keep reader interest and to avoid the editor's "tightening" pen. If your letter gets shortened, it will probably be in the last paragraphs. Stick to one issue. The letters that most frequently get printed are short, concise, to the point. Stay focused. Write your letter in pithy, clever statements, but remember that this is not easy to do! You will probably need to write several drafts of your letter to condense your message. Two or three paragraphs is recommended. Long, wordy letters give the impression that you're having to work hard to get your point across.

- **Check the newspaper's guidelines for submissions**. Most papers want letters of 200 to 250 words. That's not much, which makes the above point that much more important. Besides, in our Internet-and-microwave age, people scan more than they read in depth. Some papers may insist on e-mail submissions (that way they can cut and paste and other editing is easier also) and others will accept both digital and paper copy.

- **Mention your credentials if you have them**. It's fine to comment as an ordinary citizen, but if you happen to be an accountant, your objections to the new state budget will carry more weight with both the editor and the reader.

- **Include your name, address, e-mail address, and phone number at the top of your letter.** Editors often require this information because they will need to verify your identity. You can state that this information is not to be published if you wish but there is a chance that your paper won't publish anonymous letters.

- **Oops, I almost forgot: if you're a minor, give your age.** This is one more feature that draws attention and adds a bit of color. Especially if you're writing on an issue that people don't expect young folks to be interested in, you will make an extra impression. If you happen to be writing on topics related to education, you will be either a positive or negative advertisement for home education depending on what you say and how well you say it.

- **State the problem and the solution.** Don't just say, "Governor McSwine has failed to protect the citizens' freedom." Say, "Remember Tuesday is election day and cast your vote for John Goodguy. His character and his record are what our state needs today." Don't attack people — attack stands and opinions. Be a Christian lady or gentleman and yet be forceful (admittedly, this will take some practice). Ranting or ending every sentence with an exclamation point will get you disregarded, if you get published at all.

- **Include proof if possible.** If you can give a brief fact that validates your opinion, or quote a statistic or number that applies, this will add persuasiveness.

- **Consider an op-ed piece.** Newspapers sometimes accept full-length pieces by readers for publication. If you can't do justice to your topic in a three-paragraph letter to the editor, then contact the paper for their guidelines for op-ed articles and submit one.

- **Proofread, proofread, proofread.** And have a few other people read it, too, for grammar, style, and content.

So there are ways you can get your message out through publications that are already in existence. In fact, by writing a letter to the editor you may get a conservative viewpoint articulated in a liberal paper. Think about it.

Maybe you should have your own talk radio program. All you'd have to do is find some businesses that agree with your viewpoint and are willing to buy advertising from you to pay the radio station for your airtime. Depending on the station, it might be cheaper than you would think.

Then there's the option of starting a publication of your own. If you don't have several million to start your own TV station or newspaper, there's always the Internet. Get a good book on blogging and you'll be amazed at the potential of a blog to get a message out to lots of people.

Endnotes

1. http://historysstory.blogspot.com/search?q=january+30+tet+offensive.
2. http://topics.nytimes.com/top/reference/timestopics/people/c/walter_cronkite/index.html.
3. http://en.wikipedia.org/wiki/Daisy_(advertisement).
4. Reuters News Service, Sept. 20, 2006.
5. en.wikipedia.org/wiki/Ted_Turner.

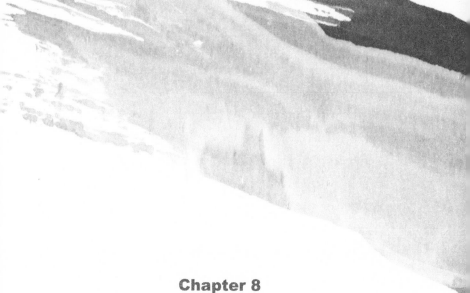

Chapter 8

THE ARTS

Why a chapter about the arts in a book about restoring Christian principles to American culture? Because art is a powerful force in our culture. It tells us a lot about our culture and it helps to shape it into what it is. It can be used for great good or great evil.

What is art? The dictionary definitions are pretty general, applying to almost any activity involving creativity and skill. Cooking is sometimes called culinary art. For our purposes here, let's think in terms of the "fine arts": music, painting, drawing, sculpture, literature, dance, theater (including TV and movies), etc.

Art *expresses* what we think and feel. For instance, when Charles Wesley wrote one of his beautiful hymns, he was expressing what he thought and felt about God.

At the same time, art *influences* what we think and feel. When you sing one of those hymns, the quality theology in the lyrics helps you to *think* more truthfully about God. At the same time, the beautiful melody, complemented by supportive (not overwhelming) harmony and rhythm speaks to your spirit and generates positive emotions or *feelings* about God.

Since how we think and feel determines all our actions, that means the arts have an awful lot of power in our lives. Because it both influences and expresses what we think and feel, you can tell a lot about a society by the art it produces collectively. Nutritionists tell us, "You are what you eat." Spiritually, that could mean you are what spiritual food you eat. Or as Proverbs 23:7 tells us, "For as he thinks within himself, so he is." You are what you think.

Satan understands the power of the arts. That's why he has always been busy perverting them for his own use. Let's look at some of the marks of the enemy's influence on the arts in our day.

Sculpture: Traditionally, statues looked like something. If a sculptor made a statue of a general on a horse, it looked like a general on a horse. In our day, if you see such a statue it's an old one. The new ones are "modern art," which means that you don't know what you're looking at without reading the bronze plaque at the bottom. This represents a general modern rebellion in the arts against traditional morality and values. The underlying spiritual issue is simply that God loves design while Satan loves distortion. This also reflects the fact that we don't have heroes anymore, just role models. Hero denotes character, role model only skill. Some sports figures are role models to young athletes, but rarely are they called heroes; rarely is anyone called a hero anymore. It's as if we don't want to believe there is such a thing as excellence in character. Maybe we used to like such people as examples to follow. Now it seems we just don't want to look bad by comparison.

Painting: I read an article about how the National Endowment for the Arts had declined a beautiful new painting of Christ calming the storm. Said it was too "traditional." What they really meant was too godly. Look around at the paintings sold in stores. If they're new, they're usually ugly or indecent. That stuff wouldn't have been found on the walls of most homes a couple of generations ago. Do an online search or check out a book from the library for a look at some paintings by Norman Rockwell. You'll see how a painter can produce both superb quality and a positive cultural effect.

Poetry: Bill Clinton designated a woman named Maya Angelou as America's poet laureate when he came to office as president of the United States. I looked up some of her poetry out of curiosity. It was junk. A lot of the lines didn't rhyme (which isn't always bad — see Longfellow's *Song of Hiawatha*), the sentiments were mostly cheap and ugly, and there was no regular meter to it. You can call that artsy and creative if you want to, but read "Paul Revere's Ride" and Angelou's work will look pretty sick by comparison. I don't know her and don't want to communicate any personal disrespect for her. But there's bad poetry, good poetry, and great poetry. Longfellow's is great in my opinion; Angelou's is not. Yet she's singled out as an icon by the president.

Photography: There are some collections of great photography in the world. There's also Robert Mapplethorpe's stuff. Some of Mapplethorpe's photos were part of a traveling exhibit by the Smithsonian Institution. That means it was paid for by the taxpayer. One of his photos was so perverted that I won't describe it here, but it made the national news. Your tax dollars at work. Note: This represents one of the reasons that I talk so much about government in this book. If we can bring government under control, tax money will no longer be spent on things like art that are none of the government's business. Then stuff like Mapplethorpe's trash will never see the light of day, because nobody in his right mind would pay his own money for it.

Music: This is a biggie. Music has been perverted in so many ways that even if I was an expert, which I'm not, I couldn't begin to deal with it adequately here. But let me just note some basics, okay? First, whenever the Bible talks about music, it's always in the context of worship. Music is a form of worship. It's used in godly worship and it's used in ungodly worship, including satanic worship. It's powerful. That's why they don't play lullabies at football games. It has an effect. Music is much more than the lyrics. You can put godly words to ungodly music, but the net result is just contamination. The Bible principle is that when the clean touches the unclean, the clean becomes unclean. The unclean doesn't become clean. You want to argue about that? Convince me that you really want the truth and I'll talk to you about it. If you're not intellectually honest, I'm not going to waste my time with you. That would be casting pearls. Hint: If a question starts with "What's *wrong* with my . . ." it's usually not an honest question. Usually, it's somebody wanting to argue to justify doing what they want to do. I'll have to leave it to those better educated in music than I am, to explain the science of music and the specific elements that affect our minds, but if you have an honest heart God will lead you to the right choices.

If you claim that music is neutral and only the lyrics matter, you're either uninformed or you're not intellectually honest. If you research it you'll learn that music has been used to make cows give more and less milk, make plants grow faster or slower and even die. Music has been used in experiments on mice that were then timed working their way through a maze. A control group of mice heard no music. The "rock mice" were the slowest to find their way through the maze. The "classical mice" went through the fastest. The no-music mice were in between. In an autopsy afterward, the rock mice had developed weird growths on their brains.[1] The high school student who did the experiment in his basement said that he had to cut it short because the "rock mice" killed each other. Oh yeah, music is neutral. Stop kidding yourself.

Music can be bad because of lyrics, of course. Remember, we're looking for that which is excellent. Some lyrics express bad values. Some aren't true. Some are vulgar. I shouldn't have to tell you that such rot is not fit for a Christian. Do you really want to fill your only brain with the words and the sound of hard rock or rap? Don't waste your time and expose your mind to garbage. As you think, so you will be (Prov. 23:7).

Contemporary Christian music (CCM) is the choice of most young believers I know. I won't condemn the whole genre, because some of it is great. The listener needs to be discerning. The vast majority of it that I've heard, however, is either weak on lyrical protein (usually me-centered rather than saying much about God) or dominated by beat to the point where the melody is almost concealed. That's backward. Just because it makes you feel good doesn't mean you're worshiping. Choose with care.

Literature: Again, the old stuff usually is still around because it's good. Newer books that are hailed as "modern classics" are usually trash. *Tobacco Road* would qualify for that title, in my opinion. But being old doesn't necessarily mean good. I think Nathaniel Hawthorne's work reeks to high heaven. Oh, he was an expert writer. But what did he write? Everything of his that they made me read in school was all gloom and doom and depression. If you know of something he wrote that's uplifting, let me know.

If we want to think, feel, and *be* what God wants us to think, feel, and be, we have to go to Scripture for some principles to evaluate the arts. You could spend years doing that, but because of limited space (not to mention my limited intelligence) we'll look at just a couple of passages.

> And this I pray, that your love may abound still more and more in real knowledge and all discernment, so that you may approve the things that are excellent, in order to be sincere and blameless until the day of Christ (Phil. 1:9–10).

Read that again, slowly and carefully. Paul prays for the Philippians to have a love that abounds more and more in two things, knowledge and discernment. Knowledge is just a collection of facts. Information. But discernment speaks of a skill: the ability to tell one thing from another. Paul wants them to have love, knowledge, and discernment for a very important reason. That reason is that they may be able to approve the things that are excellent.

I looked up the Greek word translated into "excellent" here, and it basically means outstanding from all the rest. Paul wants his people to be able not just to tell the difference between good and bad, but from good and best. That's an important skill. To use literature for an example, think of how many books there are in the world. Do you have time to read all the good books? Or will you have to search out only the best to keep from wasting part of your life? It's the same with music, movies, etc.

The other passage we'll consider is Philippians 4:8:

> Finally, brethren, whatever is true, whatever is honorable, whatever is right, whatever is pure, whatever is lovely, whatever is of good repute, if there is any excellence and if anything worthy of praise, dwell on these things.

Paul begins with *truth*. When looking at or listening to art, the Christian should ask, "Is this really true?" Does life genuinely operate in this fashion in light of God's revelation? This automatically eliminates most of what is called "Impressionist painting." For instance, Picasso was a great artist who could paint beautifully. But he is remembered for his "impressionist" work. That work should have been called "distortionist" work. His impressionist paintings are barely recognizable as what they are supposed to represent. Did Picasso use a ton of talent and skill in producing those works? Yes. Are they an accurate reproduction of the God-made subjects they represented? No.

The second word is *honorable*. It speaks of *honor* or *dignity*. You could evaluate a lot of song lyrics with this one. Using Wesley or Isaac Watts for comparison, not many of the new Christian songs we sing in church have much dignity. These guys wrote for an exalted God with exalted words. It was real poetry.

The third key to aesthetic comprehension has to do with the moral dimension — what is *right*. Some art makes a moral statement and it should be considered with rightness or wrongness in mind. That brings us to the next concept.

Purity is the fourth word. It also speaks of morality — contrasting that which is clean, chaste, innocent, and pure from that which is impure, squalid, sordid, and defiled. This condemns most movies made in recent years. It also blasts country music. Though a small percentage of country songs express sentiments that are patriotic, religious, or otherwise commendable, most country music themes are adultery, alcohol abuse, fornication and the ever-present self-pity. Cry babies.

Next comes beauty. Whatever is *lovely*. If you bring this up in conversation, some non-thinking individual is sure to quack the old adage: "Beauty is in the eye of the beholder!" No, that's a lie. Beauty is in the eye of the Creator. We may not always be able to discern it, but it is a matter of discernment, not proof. That's why Paul prayed for that skill for his followers. We may not always recognize beauty, but God does or He would never have placed it in this list. If beauty is in the eye of the beholder then there is really no beauty in the world at all.

The sixth concept, that of *good repute*, reflects the public testimony of the art and the artist. Some bad people are skillful enough to produce quality in some respects, and some bad art contains some good parts. The idea here seems to be searching out that which is agreed on as good, by people who are good.

Excellence is word number seven. It's a comparative term that demonstrates that some things are better than others. Some things are bad, some things are good, some things are excellent. The focus is on quality, which deserves to be considered carefully. One sure sign of quality is that it is durable. It lasts. Beware of anything contemporary. It may be very good. On the other hand, it may not. In any case, it hasn't yet passed the test of time. Great art lasts.

The last concept is general. *Anything worthy of praise.* We're reminded that some things merit praise and some things don't. Paul closes the verse by saying that we should let our minds dwell on these things.

Note that Paul never says in these verses to think about things that we like. He never says it's okay to think about things that make us feel good. That's because beauty really isn't in the eye of the beholder. We can decide we like something, but only God decides what we should like. The world needs to see and hear from Christians committed to art for the glory of God, not our own pleasure.

So get involved in the arts. Get yourself a better education than I did. Do a little research and learn what is good art and what isn't. Then go looking for your place in the arts. It may just be as a consumer, a reader of good books and listener of good music. Or it may be as a producer of good art. Maybe you like playing an instrument and could perform for others in a God-glorifying way. Maybe you could get some friends together and start a chorus group or an orchestra. You could play in retirement homes, nursing homes, schools, and on the children's ward of the local hospital. All this is ministry if done right.

You may think, *Oh, I could never take on a project like that. Who would help me? How could I finance it?* You know something? God can pay for what He orders. Just seek His will and push forward with determination.

I'll leave you with an anecdote for a little encouragement. You remember the movie *Fireproof*? It was made by a church in Georgia. It cost only $500,000. That's a pittance in the movie business, but it was a box office smash. So was their previous movie, *Facing the Giants*. But it only cost them $100,000. But that wasn't their first movie. The first one they made was called *Flywheel*. It cost them *$20,000*. A lot of churches and other groups could manage that. So don't despise the day of small beginnings.

Endnotes

1. http://www.edu-cyberpg.com/Music/Mice_and_Music_Experiment_Mo.html.

Chapter 9

THE FAMILY

You don't need me to tell you that the American family is in trouble. Satan knows how important the family is to God and His Church, so he attacks it constantly from every direction. Some of his attacks are obvious, such as the flood of pornography on the Internet. Some attacks are less obvious, like the feminization of our boys in school (see *The War Against Boys* by Christina Hoff Sommers). But all things considered, no aspect of our culture is being bombarded with hostility like the family.

I grew up in a dysfunctional family. My parents couldn't help it; they weren't Christians at the time and neither of them had good parenting models in their own parents. My dad had a drinking problem to complicate matters. When I was about 11 years old, I was admitted to the hospital for three days of testing to find out the cause of my persistent abdominal pains. It was concluded that they were caused by chronic stress. I'm a living testimony that a home full of strife is no environment for a little kid to thrive in.

Most likely, your home is a far cry from the one I grew up in. I'm targeting this book at Christian homeschool youth, and if that describes you, you are most likely a very blessed young person. One of the neatest things about my job is that it takes me on speaking engagements to homeschool conferences all over America and around the world. At every one, I have the pleasure of seeing moms and dads and kids being together and enjoying it. No homeschool family is perfect, but on average they're a far cry from what I see in my own neighborhood and most places I go. What an encouragement it is to me when I hear moms speaking lovingly to their little ones instead of snarling in irritation. And what a blessing to see sharp, mature teenagers who dress as if they have some respect for themselves and for their parents' reputation. The cool thing about it is that it's everywhere. I spoke at the Japanese national homeschool conference a few years ago, and even though I couldn't understand a thing the parents and kids were saying to each other, their behavior and tone of voice told the story eloquently. I was among Christian homeschoolers.

God bless the family. The world around us seems to be disintegrating, with destruction and misery everywhere. People are addicted to drugs, alcohol, gangsta rap. Gangs beat up and kill people just because of the color of the clothes they happen to be wearing. Sexually transmitted disease runs rampant, lives all around us display frustration, boredom, confusion, insecurity, and fear. But once in a while you see a family that works, and it floods you with renewed hope for the world.

This book is a summons to rise up. It's a bugle call. And just as Nehemiah's men sounded the trumpet to call warriors to the place on the wall where the attack was coming, I want to call your attention to what Satan is doing to the family in our day. Nobody can fight on every battlefield in the culture, but we all must fight the battle for the family. Here are some of the weapons the enemy is wielding against us. Prepare yourself to deal with them.

Feminism

Radical feminism is a child of the Communist movement. Remember, Communists are revolutionaries and revolution is about overthrowing the established culture and replacing it with something new. Since the family is God's main channel for passing on values and morals from one generation to another, revolutionaries want to destroy it so that they can stop that generational torch from being passed and teach their own values to the rising generation of children. Revolutionary feminists preach that America is a male-dominated place in which women are oppressed. They tell women that they are equal to men in every way (which isn't true — in some ways women are far superior) and therefore should claim an identical role with them. They were the ones who agitated for women in combat, one of the most misguided ideas to ever come along. Feminism preaches that women cannot be fulfilled as wives and mothers. They need a "real" career as well. They have been successful in brainwashing the Church to the point that most Christian girls believe that. Male-bashing has become so entrenched in our society that men are sometimes hesitant to act like men. Some of us have been growled at by women because we tried to hold a door for them, as if it was an insult to their strength rather than a gesture of honor.

If you're a guy, be a man and make no apologies for it. That's what any girl should be looking for. If you're a girl, be a Proverbs 31 woman. She put her family first and her husband and children praised her for it. If you read the statistics showing how many working women are leaving the business world to come home, you'll get a sense of how unfulfilling feminism for some is proving to be.

Pornography

You cannot escape pornography unless you live in an underground bunker with no electricity. It's all over the airwaves and saturates the Internet. It's on billboards and in newspaper advertising. People differ on their definitions of what constitutes porn, but I don't know anybody who denies that it's everywhere. If anybody does deny it, he must be blind. Some people distinguish between "soft porn" and "hardcore porn" but don't bother to debate it. If it contains an image of the human body with the intent to stimulate a sexual response, call it porn.

Men are much more susceptible to pornography because they are wired to observe. A man can find a woman very attractive without ever having met her personally. Because love and sex were designed to work together, a man who is distracted by skimpily dressed women in person or in a picture is giving emotional energy to a fantasy that should be dedicated to his wife. A woman can sense this and that is why many a husband has been surprised by the violent reaction of his wife when she catches him glancing at another woman or a picture of one. He thinks he was just looking. She knows somebody is stealing something that belongs to her and she is deeply wounded by it. Then when she reacts and grows less responsive to her husband's love because of the hurt, he gets wounded and has to deal with guilt at the same time. A lot of marriages have broken up because of pornography. Lust is a man's constant battle. Don't take it lightly.

The Homosexual Movement

Make no mistake about it, the so-called gay rights movement is not about anything right. It's about destroying the family. The liberal media and even liberal churches are working hand-in-hand to advance an agenda in the name of gay rights that will destroy many real rights if it is successful. We hear so much about discrimination against gays that we lose sight of the fact that homosexuality is condemned in Scripture. Whenever somebody commits a crime against somebody because he is homosexual, the news blows it up to make it sound like a civil rights issue. The brutal beating murder of Matthew Shephard a few years ago was noised abroad. Shrill cries went up for hate crimes legislation. That is a testament to our modern incapability of sustaining logical thought. Some people can't see that a person who is murdered because of his race, sexual preference, or religion is no more or less dead than somebody who was killed with a motive of robbery. The traditional (and Constitutional) American approach to crime and punishment was to "make the punishment fit the crime." No consideration was given to the reason somebody was killed. A person had been murdered and the murderer was expected to pay a price whether he murdered out of greed, anger, prejudice, or whatever. The push for hate crimes legislation is an attempt to further legitimize homosexuality in the public attitude by tying it to civil rights in the public mind. Are the lives of people who were murdered out of revenge any less important than the lives of those who were murdered out of prejudice?

If the homosexual lobby is successful in establishing gay "marriage" it will be devastating to society. If two "gay" men can get married and receive the legal benefits of marriage, then two heterosexual roommates in the college dorm can do the same. They can date all the girls they want, and get divorced from each other when they decide they want real marriages. In addition, gay marriage would destroy any legal protection that real marriage has as a cultural institution. If we legalize marriage between two men or two women, on what grounds could we deny a man's right to marry three women, or a woman to marry multiple men? Or a brother's right to marry his sister? Make no mistake, if "gay marriage" is legalized, any perversion of marriage will be right behind.

School

There is a subtle dynamic at work when children spend the most and the best of their waking hours giving their attention and obedience to professional strangers rather than their parents. Children have a natural respect for those who teach them, and it's not surprising when parents say one thing and their child contradicts them with, "But my teacher said. . . ." The other side of the coin is peer pressure. I was thoroughly peer dependent long before I reached high school, and I wasn't the only one. Most of us viewed our parents as "out of it." Our younger siblings were dorks. Our friends were the ones whose approval we craved the most.

Besides the "two masters" effect and peer dependency, school curriculum is an enemy of the family as well. Two anti-family books that have been introduced in recent years are *Heather Has Two Mommies* and *King and King*. You won't have much trouble guessing what they're about.

The antagonism of the school toward the family isn't completely unintentional. A president of the Chicago Teachers Union once railed against parents and others who were trying to give some input into school policy: "We don't tell them what to do in their kitchens, so why should they tell us what to do in our classrooms?"[1] Frenzied applause came from her audience of school employees, but it didn't reflect well on the intelligence of either speaker or listeners. In our kitchens, we're not cooking her meals nor is her money buying the groceries. In their classrooms, they are working on our children and being paid with our tax dollars. If they don't see the difference, we've got the wrong people calling themselves educators.

Media/Entertainment

When I was a kid, there was actually a prime time TV series titled *Father Knows Best*. *My Three Sons*, *Leave It to Beaver*, *The Donna Reed Show*, and other programs also painted a picture of family life that spoke of love, security, stability, and joy. Now we get *The Simpsons*, *Beavis and Butthead*, and *Two-and-a-Half Men*. Many programs feature two young people living together apart from marriage, and if they portray a family at all it's a dysfunctional one, usually with a moron for a father.

In those days even secular music featured themes of love, fidelity, and marriage. Now the radio waves bring us violence and sexual exploitation. The dark side of the electronic age.

Government

This topic is too big to do justice to here. Government damages families in a million ways, most of them sneaky. The inheritance tax, for instance, steals from the family a big chunk of what the deceased parents worked for and wanted to leave to their children. Welfare policies that encourage having babies out of wedlock have contributed to the fact that around 40 percent of the children in our country are born into fatherless families. Government dictates what kind of safety seats children ride in, certification standards for their teachers, and how their parents may and may not administer discipline. Add to this an overall burden of federal, state, and local taxation that makes it very hard today to live on one income, forcing many moms into the workplace and kids into daycare. All this is just the tip of the iceberg, so take warning. The government is gradually taking ownership of your family and will steal more and more of its life unless it is stopped.

The Birth Dearth

Until about 1900, people acted as if they really believed that children are a blessing as the Bible clearly says. The average American family numbered seven living children, despite the much higher infant mortality rate. But early in the 20th century the enemy of our souls was making a sneak attack on the culture of family. He raised up leaders who taught women to be dissatisfied with the role of wife and mom. He fronted people like Margaret Sanger, founder of Planned Parenthood, who believed that humans were no better than animals and their numbers should be controlled. Sanger and her allies had cut their activist teeth in the eugenics movement. Eugenics is the "science" of selective breeding of humans for the purpose of weeding out "inferior" humans and eliminating them from the gene pool. It is no coincidence that the vast majority of Planned Parenthood clinics even today are located in minority neighborhoods. To quote her own words, eugenics should be used to produce "children from the fit, less from the unfit. That is the aim of birth control." She thought she and her people had the right to plan the human race. She proposed to use "birth control to create a race of thoroughbreds."[2] Just like Hitler's plan to dominate the world with his super race.

But not too many little thoroughbreds! Sanger preached legal abortion, limited family size, and once said, "The kindest thing a large family can do for its youngest member is to kill it."[3]

It's strange and tragic that she was so successful that a hundred years later, society has embraced the idea of smaller families. When was the last time you heard a sermon extolling the blessings of a large family? Don't hold your breath. We all claim that children are a blessing. Yet nobody wants too many of those blessings.

There are several kinds of blessings mentioned in Scripture. They include wealth, long life, good health, wisdom, a close relationship with God, victory over enemies, peace of mind, and a "quiver full" of children (see Psalm 127:5). Look, I didn't write it, I just read it, okay? So how many times have you prayed to tell God you had enough wealth, so please don't send any more? Or that you already have all the good health you want, so you'd like to be sick for a while? Or that you were tired of walking close to Him and would rather go it alone for a year or two? Honestly, I can't think of very many blessings that believers want to limit. But with kids, it's different. We've been sold a bill of goods by godless philosophies and now we stop at two children just like everybody else. Just like the world.

Instead of hearing sermons about how great it is to have a houseful of children, if we hear the topic addressed at all it's an exhortation to use wisdom in our family planning. Don't have more children than you can cope with. (I thought you "coped" with cancer, not with children.) Never a word about how God might be able to handle the family planning on His own.

This is just one example but a pretty clear one, I think. The Church has come to accept an idea from the world even though logic would say that children are a blessing biblically so we should want more. We take our cues from the world rather than from an honest examination of God's Word. The Muslims know better. Some of them are moving to Europe where their families average six or seven children and the non-Muslim families average one or two. It's estimated that England and France will be Muslim countries within 20 or 30 years by immigration and propagation. I'm thankful that in America homeschoolers are having larger families than the average. It's a sign of good things to come.

That's a very sketchy overview of the battle for the family.

What can I do?

1. Pray. God loves the family. He invented it. He wants it to thrive more than you and I do. Pray for your own families, for families in your church and your neighborhood.

2. Write to your elected officials about family issues. Take your whole family to lobby your legislators if possible. Write letters to the editor with documentation to prove your viewpoint. Don't let the radicals control the print media.

3. Protect your purity. Start your own family right by getting married with no regrets and no spiritual or emotional baggage.

4. When you get married, let God do the family planning. If He gives you a child who needs all the attention of both parents, He will give you only that one. If He gives you a bigger quiver (Ps. 127:5 KJV), that means it's your job to train an army. Make them a horde for the Lord.

5. Fight the moral issues such as pornography and adult book stores. Research your city and county laws to make sure immoral activities aren't going on in violation of code.

6. Resolve to educate your own children in godliness and patriotism as well as academics.

7. Prepare financially for your future marriage. Don't start married life with financial pressure. It will distract you and your spouse from all the great things about family life.

Endnotes

1. *Chicago Tribune*, May 23, 1988.

2. www.freerepublic.com/focus/news/2401714/posts-Cached.

3. http://www.freerepublic.com/focus/news/2401714/posts.

Chapter 10

THE CHURCH

I'm a little hesitant about writing this chapter because it requires me to say some hard things about the modern Church. Please don't take offense at any person or idea or practice that I express criticism of, just because I say so. Instead, look at what I say objectively. First, examine my ideas in light of Scripture and see if they line up. Then, look around you at your own church and other churches you're familiar with and see if what I've said rings true with your own experience. Don't take anything I say on my own authority. I can be wrong.

Above all, understand that I love the Church and wish her all blessings. The fact that I criticize her doesn't mean that I don't care about her. It means I do. I love my children, too; I love them too much to see them go astray without calling their attention to the problem. So listen to my assessment of the problems, my proposed solutions, and decide for yourself what you need to do.

My first premise, the one that will guide what I say in this chapter, is that I believe the American Church today is in apostasy. Someone has described the difference between apostasy and revival this way:

> Revival is a time when the Church influences the world.
> Apostasy is a time when the world influences the Church.

I say that today the Church is following the world's lead rather than vice versa. Our attitudes, values, habits, dress, speech, and entertainments all bear the image of the world and the worldly man.

Keep this theme in mind as we move forward here. In the pages that follow, I'm going to talk about the problems in the American Church. I hope you have the courage and honesty of heart to examine my beliefs objectively and match them against the teachings of Scripture even if they make you uncomfortable.

God's Church is beautiful. I love my local church and I love the universal Church, the Body of Christ everywhere in the world. I've been to several other countries in Europe, Asia, and North America, and the Church is the Church everywhere. When I speak to conference attendees in other states and other countries, nearly all of them are Christians. That's not surprising, as I always approach the topics I speak on from a biblical perspective. And I always feel a kinship with the people in my audience. They are believers in the Lord Jesus Christ and we are family.

So when I harp on the problems and failures of the Church, don't get the idea that I don't love the Church or that I am mad at her. It's just that we have to recognize our problems before we can search out the answers to them. It wouldn't be an act of love for a doctor to pretend his patient wasn't sick. It is love to recognize that there is a problem, discern what is causing it, and apply the best treatment. I believe that the Church in America is very sick today and that the answer is not to ignore it. Neither is the answer to condemn the Church or give up on her and try, as many people have, to replace her with government programs, social organizations, bureaucracies, or para-church ministries. Nope, she's still God's Church and she will always be His chosen instrument in reaching the world with the gospel.

So as we look at the Church in this chapter, let's be honest with ourselves regarding our failings and yet stay positive in our search for solutions. The Church can be healed and made once again the city on a hill for the rest of society.

Of course there are zillions of different types of churches. Each has its own individual personality and inner culture, just as do nuclear families as part of extended families. Brother Joe grows up and marries. He runs his family a little differently than does brother Jed, who marries and leads his home similarly but with a slightly different flavor than Joe's. They are still blood kin, but unique members of the larger family. I've seen it with my four married children. No problem.

Unfortunately, the extended church family in the United States is in serious trouble. Local churches look like each other to a certain extent, and that's good. What concerns me is that they look so much like the world outside the Church.

The churches that are looked to as examples for other churches are usually what we call megachurches. They are large, well-financed, and up-to-date technologically. Their preachers exude charisma and professionalism. They are usually highly educated and have advanced academic degrees. Their sermons, and sometimes their entire morning services, are broadcast on radio and television. Some of these men are well-known in secular society even as they are in Christian circles.

None of these characteristics are bad. Did you hear what I just said? None of these things are bad. There's nothing wrong with getting your message on TV and radio. There's nothing wrong with a leader who has a winning personality. There's nothing wrong with having abundant financial resources to get the job done. What's wrong with the American Church today is not that we have these things in our churches or desire to have them. It is that we have come to *depend* on them. We have come to depend on them because we lack something else.

The advantages I just listed are all material resources. They're fine in their place. That is, their own place. They are not fine as substitutes for spiritual resources. Money, technology, and talent can be wonderfully useful tools, but we're doomed if we think they can replace spiritual resources such as faith, humility, personal evangelism, family unity, good works, and the power of the Holy Spirit.

Generally speaking, leaders in the modern Church have taken it upon themselves to build the Church for Jesus. That's why there's so much emphasis on numbers in attendance and membership. The problem with that is that Jesus would rather build it Himself. In Matthew 16:18 He told Peter that "upon this rock I will build my church; and the gates of hell shall not prevail against it" (KJV). So it is Christ's job to build the Church, not the pastor's or the Church's job. When we try to do His job for Him, we create problems.

That's the undergirding principle in the disaster of the "seeker sensitive" movement we see all around us today. We want larger churches, so we try to attract "seekers" into the Church. To do that, we use methods and messages that we hope will "reach the new generation." We jettison tradition and become trendy in hopes that we can offer worldly people an experience that they will like and want to come back for again and again. Many churches have succeeded in this. The result? They're full of worldly people.

Please understand that I'm not questioning the motives of church leaders who see this issue differently than I do. Many of them love the Lord and love people. They're very sincere. They're trying to get the job done for Jesus. God bless them. I'm just questioning the priorities and methods. How do they stack up against Scripture and the lessons learned throughout two thousand years of Church history?

Should We Dump Tradition?

Okay, buckle your seatbelt because at this point we're about to encounter some turbulence that will stretch your brain a bit. I'm going to ask you to think harder than most people are comfortable with. You're training to be a leader, remember? Hard thinking is part of a leader's job. So suck it up.

You already know that the American Church today is trying to find a balance between the traditional and the contemporary. Some churches have a contemporary service and a traditional service, too. What should we do? Have both kinds to suit older and younger worshipers? Or is one truly better than the other, meaning we should dump one and embrace the other? Or are we just in a natural transition from the old way to the new way? How do we decide?

I've not yet heard a clear explanation of why we're moving away from old church practices to new ones. The usual answer is, "We're trying to reach the new generation." But nobody seems to know exactly who the new generation is, or when their generation started. After all, new people are born every year. And what does it mean to "reach" them? Are they reached when they start attending church regularly? When they get saved? And is there research or experience to show how people are supposed to be reached? How do we know if we're doing the right thing? Are we doing new things just because they're new? Does this make any more sense than doing old things just because they're old?

Let's start out by agreeing on one thing: There is nothing deader than dead tradition. Doing something just because we've always done it that way makes no sense. Reminds me of a story I heard about a young wife fixing her first roast beef dinner. As she prepared to put the roast in the pan, she took out a big knife and cut off the end of it. As she did so, she realized that her mother had always done the same thing. Curious, she stuck the pan in the oven and picked up the phone to call her mom and ask why she always cut the end off a roast before cooking it. Mom didn't know, except that she had always seen Grandma do it that way. So the two of them asked Grandma about it the next time they went to dinner at her house. She didn't remember either, but she had always done it that way. Really curious now, the three of them drove to the nursing home to visit Great-grandma. Oh yes, she said, she remembered always doing that. They pressed her for the reason, wondering where the tradition had come from. Simple, Great-grandma replied. Her roasting pan had been too short.

That family had a tradition that had grown up by accident and wasn't based on any real reason. No harm in throwing that one out. But is that always the case?

America's national birth came about because of tradition. We tend to refer to the founders as revolutionaries and even call the War of Independence a revolution. They called it that themselves, but by definition it was anything but. A revolution is the overthrowing of an old system and the installment of a new one. The patriots of early

America were not trying to create a new way of life, but to protect a way of life that had grown up on their continent for over 150 years. King George and Parliament were passing laws that deprived the colonies of their rights as English citizens. That was something new. In fact, it was a violation of English common law, which had a history of several centuries.

It was said that the common law had existed from "time immemorial." They meant that it had been built up by slow refinements down through the ages. It was a mixture of judicial decisions, parliamentary decrees, unwritten custom, agreements, and grants by the kings. It added up to an enormous list of precedents, all of which had for centuries been diligently studied and applied by English courts and lawyers. Teachers of the common law boasted of its traditional nature. They pointed out that ideas tested by centuries of human experience were a lot more dependable than somebody's brand-new "bright idea." No one king or Parliament, they believed, could toss out the common law and start over to please themselves. British statesman Edmund Burke said, "I prefer the collected wisdom of the ages to the abilities of any two men living. . . . We are afraid to put men to live and trade each on his own private stock of reason; because we suspect that . . . individuals would do better to avail themselves of the general bank and capital of nations and ages."[1] Makes sense.

Legal scholar Sir Edward Coke agreed: "Our days upon the earth are but a shadow in respect to the old ancient days and times past, wherein the laws have been by the wisdom of many excellent men . . . by long and continued experience, fined and refined, what no man . . . in any one age would ever have been effected or attained to."[2] In other words, tradition offers the collected knowledge and experience of many generations, which are much more likely to be wise than the speculations of any man or group of men at any given time. So when in doubt, the scales of decision should be weighted in favor of tradition over trendiness.

See, I told you this would be a brain stretcher.

One more quote, this one from British Chief Justice Hale: "It is reasonable for me to prefer a law by which a kingdom hath been happily governed four or five hundred years than to adventure [risk] this happiness and peace of a kingdom upon some theory of my own. . . . Long experience makes more discoveries . . . than it is possible for the wisest council of men at first to foresee."[3]

Are you gutsy enough to take this line of reasoning a little further? Let's test it on church practices. Try out your mental courage and honesty by looking at church music. Most of the music used in most churches I've attended recently is new. Why is it there? Is it better music? Does it please God more to hear it sung than the old songs? Is there an automatic advantage to new music over old?

It's not because there was a shortage of music. Isaac Watts wrote over 600 songs. Charles Wesley wrote over 6,000. Fanny Crosby, over 8,000. That's just three writers. And all three are still popular today. Must have done something write . . . I mean, right. So I think it's safe to say that there have been hundreds of thousands of Christian songs written more than 50 years ago. Call that traditional church music. We're not using new stuff because there's a shortage of the old.

Are we using new music because it has better lyrical content? Not most of what I've heard. A lot of that is "seven-eleven" music: the same seven-word phrase sung eleven times. Much of the rest of it isn't necessarily repetitive but the lyrics are shallow. Often it's "me-centered" rather than God-centered: Oh, Jesus, I love You so much, I'm really devoted to You, I live for You, I worship You. . . .

Wow. Makes me sound pretty good, but doesn't say much about Jesus.

Now consider the lyrics of some God-centered music.

> Immortal, invisible, God only wise,
> In light inaccessible, hid from our eyes,
> Most gracious, most glorious, the Ancient of Days,
> Almighty, victorious, Thy great name we praise.

See the difference? The first song is more about the worshiper. The second one is about God. This is not to say that there's anything wrong with "testimony" songs that speak about the things God has done in our lives. Not at all. What I'm saying is that there is a difference between songs and we can't assume that a song is good because it mentions the Lord. It must exalt Him above everything else.

What I'm NOT saying is that there is no good new music. I'm also not saying that we shouldn't write new music. After all, old music was new at one time. My purpose is to say that God deserves the best music we can bring to worship with us. And the best is more likely to be found among hundreds of thousands of songs that have stood the test of time than among a few hundred written by a modern church whose spiritual temperature is not particularly hot.

Is your brain blowing fuses yet?

Remember, revival is when the Church influences the world, and apostasy is when the world influences the Church. Also remember that it was Communist leader Friedrich Engels (now he was a *real* revolutionary) who said that if a people are *separated from their roots* they are more easily persuaded. And Charles Darwin taught us that the new form of anything is always an improvement over the old form. These ideas became embedded in the curriculum and culture of the public schools, from which most Christians of today graduated. They have infiltrated the Church. That's apostasy. Bear that in mind when you think about throwing out an old church custom in favor of something trendy. Think critically, not reactively.

Dressing up for church is a tradition. Is it based on any real purpose? Or did it just come about because people liked to show off their nice clothes?

Not entirely. It came about because there used to be an idea called "reverence." You wore the best that you had because you were trying to express reverence for God, for the time of public worship, and for the place that had been built and dedicated to Him. I recall old Grover Smith leading the singing in my grandparents' country church, standing up front in his bib overalls. He probably didn't have a suit. He was an old Ozark hill farmer and he normally dressed in bib overalls. On Sunday he wore the best he had — his best pair of bib overalls.

I used to think that the idea of sacredness attached to physical things and places was an Old Testament idea that had outlived its purpose. The main worship room is an auditorium, not a sanctuary. Just as the church is the people, not the building. But then I heard a series of sermons on the Christian and the arts that pointed out the tremendous time, skill, and expense that were invested in the building of the tabernacle, the ark of the covenenant, and the Temple. The preacher pointed out that God had people go to a lot of trouble to create an environment conducive to corporate worship. Maybe environment is more important than I thought. . . .

Then there is the idea of devoted things. Devoted means consecrated or set apart for a special purpose. It means that the communion table is not a bench to be sat on during youth meetings. It means that the offering plates are not Frisbees. Why? I've come to believe that God attaches spiritual significance to physical things that are *specifically designed for the purpose of worship* and used exclusively for that. It's certainly clear in the Old Testament. In 2 Samuel 6 it tells about a priest named Uzzah who was struck dead instantly because he touched the ark. He was trying to steady it to keep it from falling off the ox cart on which it was traveling. But God had given specific instructions concerning the ark, and it was so holy that it was not to be touched by the hand of man. It reminds you of the Holy of Holies, which could only be entered by the High Priest, and only once a year. God has attached significance to some things that we don't always understand. Maybe it's part of His training us to trust His judgment more than our own.

When I was young I had a major problem with that line of thinking. I was tired of being made to do things that I didn't want to do and that didn't make any sense. All through school and later in the military, I was drilled in obedience simply for the sake of obedience. So while still a young man I began to look for reasons for what I was required to do, and if I couldn't see the sense in it, I resented being forced to do it. There was an element of rebellion in it, and that's bad. But there was something else in it, too, and that was a desire to take responsibility for my own opinions. To figure out what was right and good and act accordingly. That's a good thing, and that desire has served me well in learning how to think outside the box and go against the flow of popular thinking.

But the next step in that growth process is to realize that while I am responsible for my own opinions, God knows things that I don't. It took a little time to adjust to that. I had been too gullible at first, and I overreacted by becoming too independent. With time and experience I'm learning to find a balance. Now I try to think independently, but with respect for the wisdom of others and a sense of the limits of my own ability and information resources.

Sometimes I don't see the reason for something but eventually come to understand it. Poor old Uzzah thought it was the most logical thing in the world to steady the ark so it wouldn't fall off the cart. But he failed to understand God's concern about His own holiness.

So I encourage you to evaluate traditions in music, dress, and other areas with an honest mind. Remember that if any idea has been kept around for centuries it usually means that it has served a purpose well. The Bible has some things to say about rebuilding the "age-old foundations" instead of forming new ones (Isa. 58:12) and seeking the "ancient paths" (Jer. 18:15). Listen to Jeremiah's lament:

> Thus says the LORD, "Stand by the ways and see and ask for the ancient paths, where the good way is, and walk in it; and you shall find rest for your souls. But they said, 'We will not walk in it' " (Jer. 6:16).

Let me illustrate this. When Booker T. Washington built Tuskegee Institute, he didn't at first build brick walks between buildings. He waited until the students had made their own paths, seeking out the quickest route between buildings, and trampled the grass along the way. Then Booker had those paths dug out a few inches and bricks laid there. No more grass got stomped out because each fall the new incoming students had the advantage of the previous classes in finding the best route to go. Any freshman who thought he knew better than students of previous years lost time and got his shoes messy in the bargain.

That's the way it is with cultural traditions in society and in the Church. Most of them are based in practical usefulness. So we shouldn't change them just for the sake of trendiness. Rather, we should make slow and careful adjustments — as Tuskegee did over the years, when they built more buildings and had to establish some new paths.

So beware of dumping traditions too hastily. Sometimes you can throw out the baby with the bathwater. When my best friend Chris Klicka died a couple of years ago, I spent several of his last days with him. Sometimes several of us who were there would gather in his bedroom and sing for him. Most of what we sang was "praise and worship" music from copied sheets that were passed around the room. When Chris requested "Great Is Thy Faithfulness," it appeared that I was the only one in the room — of a dozen or so people — who knew more than the first verse. Too bad, because it's a great message.

Did you know that the hymn "A Mighty Fortress" was written by the great reformer Martin Luther and is over five hundred years old? And "Fairest Lord Jesus" is around a thousand. They must have proven to be a blessing to many generations of Christians. What a shame that we're neglecting them these days.

A tradition is also a bridge between generations. In this context, I believe there is value in singing songs that our great-grandparents sang in church. It's an excellent way of passing on values to the coming generations. Good lyrics transmit good theology from parent to child to grandchild. Beware of watering down our doctrine by conforming our music to the fashions and trends of modern society.

Leadership

As the pastor goes, so goes the church. That is more true in some churches than others, because there are variations of church leadership forms. Some churches have a senior pastor who calls the shots and whose word is law. As one old deacon put it, "He's the pastor. He does what he wants until he does wrong." Other churches have a plurality of elders who share authority and make decisions as a group. Usually, those churches still have one presiding or teaching elder who does the bulk of the preaching. Still other churches have elders who share the decision-making, teaching, and preaching equally. And there are churches in which the elders or deacons make the decisions and the pastor does the preaching but has little formal authority.

Whatever the official structure of church leadership, everything rises and falls on leadership in the church, as in any organization. If the leaders are wise and spiritual, the church body will tend that way as well. If the leaders are worldly and undisciplined, the congregation will be, too. For that reason, Satan targets church leaders for destruction above any other church member.

Every so often you hear of a well-known pastor or Christian leader who has been caught in some egregious sin. He ran off with a woman in the church or misused the church's money. It happens often enough that it wouldn't be surprising for the public to assume that preachers are all charlatans and predators.

Part of that is no doubt due to the delight the secular news media takes in seeing a Christian leader fall. They make sure it is shouted from the housetops. Also, the public's expectations of preachers are higher than for other church people, as they should be. The Bible says leaders will be held to a stricter standard (James 3:1), and they are.

But let's not forget that these leaders are wearing bull's-eyes as far as Satan is concerned. If any member of your church committed adultery, that would be very bad for the church and its ministry in the community. But if the pastor did so, it would be many times worse. Pray for your pastor and other church leaders because they are always under attack by the enemy.

I believe that another reason that church leaders fail is that many of them are not qualified for the high-profile jobs they hold. Honest people often disagree on the form of church leadership, some advocating a strong senior pastor, some a plurality of elders, and others a pure congregational rule. But we can all agree on the qualifications of those in ministry because they are made plain in 1 Timothy 3 and Titus I. You can read them for yourself, so I won't rehearse them here. Suffice it to say that if we got the right men in leadership, they would do the right things regardless of the specific design of the local church's authority structure. A strong senior pastor will do right by his own authority if he is a godly man. Multiple elders will make wise decisions together if they are godly men. Dividing the authority in the church is no protection if it is divided among men who don't belong in leadership biblically.

It is in the selection and training of leaders that much of the spiritual warfare in the Church takes place. Reform-minded believers should give a lot of attention to this if we love God's Church and want to see her prosper. In our day, Satan has been successful in getting us to view church leadership in a twisted way.

In a few denominations, pastors are assigned to churches by a higher authority at the denominational level. When a pastor resigns, retires, or dies, the choice of his successor is made outside his church. But in most conservative churches the choice of leadership remains in the local congregation. It's been very interesting to me over the years to see this done.

Usually, the church sends out word to the Bible colleges and seminaries they're associated with: We need a pastor! Resumes start flowing in to the church in a flood or a trickle. A pulpit committee goes over the resumes, weeding out those that don't seem to be a good fit at all. Then the pile is narrowed to two or three candidates who seem to be good prospects. Finally, one or all of these finalists are invited to preach a sermon or two in the church before a vote is taken. Sometimes it's a yes/no vote on one man, sometimes it's an either/or vote on two or three. In most cases, the candidates have one thing in common: They are literally or virtually strangers to the church.

What is wrong with this picture? Aren't we using a pretty sketchy process to determine our choice of a man to whom we will be entrusting the spiritual care of ourselves and our children?

In view of the practice of both Christ and the Apostles in the New Testament, this process seems pretty flawed. Mark 3:14 succinctly states the Lord's approach to training ministers: "And He appointed twelve, so that they would be with Him and that He could send them out to preach." What does He want? Men qualified to preach. How does He intend to get them? "That they should be with Him." That's what discipleship means. Those who are less qualified spend time with one who is more qualified. Jesus taught His disciples — that's what the Sermon on the Mount is all about — but He involved the disciples in the work from the very beginning. They didn't go away to Bible college for a few years and then get a job as a pastoral assistant. No, they listened to the Lord's lectures, engaged in His group discussions, watched Him preach and counsel others, and did the legwork for Him. Jesus broke the bread and fish and supplied the multiplication miracle, but the disciples directed the seating and passed out the food. They were learning on the job.

Compare that process with preacher training today. We take a young man out of his home church where the real work of the ministry is being done. We send him away for Bible college and seminary and at age 25 we put him in a pulpit telling people in their seventies and eighties how to live their lives. He hasn't raised any children yet, hasn't developed a career yet, may not even know what it's like to work a steady job and pay regular bills. Some preparation to counsel others on how to run their lives!

The modern Church has followed the ways of the secular world in this as well as many other ways. We look at academic degrees rather than spiritual maturity in selecting leadership. First Timothy 3 and Titus 1 say nothing about attending schools and getting degrees. They talk about a man's family and his character as qualifications for ministry. We should wonder what's wrong with our church when a pastor leaves after 20 years of ministry and we can't find a man in the church qualified to replace him. What was he doing all that time if not discipling his men? So now we find ourselves choosing between strangers for our new spiritual leader? That's the fruit of doing things the world's way.

The other side of the qualifications coin is the candidate's biblical qualifications. Let's say he fulfills all the church constitution's requirements for school training. Does he match up with 1 Timothy 3 and Titus 1? Is he leading his own family well? Is his marriage an accurate picture of Christ and the Church? Are his children wise and obedient? Does he have the listed character attributes? He won't have learned those just by going to school.

We need to look at the selection and training process of church leadership according to the Bible, not according to the world's institutional approach. That's how we will get men to lead us who are qualified in God's eyes and have the wisdom to guide us through the real world.

Some of you will be pastors and the wives of pastors. Please be examining the Scriptures now as you look ahead to your important ministry. Look for ways to be involved in the ministries of your local church. Get hands-on experience now and ask your pastor and other elders for guidance along the way. There's no better school than the local church.

Decisionism

Have you ever been to a big evangelistic meeting? It's an exciting event when you see thousands of people in a big stadium with loud music and energetic preaching. Then at the end comes the grand finale. An invitation is given and mobs of people go flooding down the aisle to meet counselors and pray for salvation. It's referred to traditionally as "walking the sawdust trail," a reference to times past when such meetings were held in tents and brush arbors, the aisles between benches covered with sawdust to keep them from being trampled into mud.

Come-forward invitations or "altar calls" are a relatively new feature of revival meetings that has found its way into regular church services in some denominations. Some people like them, some don't. My purpose here isn't to take one side or the other, though I myself came to Christ on just such an invitation in church. Instead, I want to point out a problem of modern evangelistic methods in general.

Did you know that the vast majority of people who profess salvation in evangelistic meetings don't go on to serve God? It's true.

I'm indebted to evangelist Ray Comfort of Living Waters Publications for the following information. It's taken from his book *God Has a Wonderful Plan for Your Life: The Myth of the Modern Message.*[4]

This book deals with a dangerous and misunderstood trend in the modern church: decisionism. I don't know if that's a real word, but if not I'll call it one. Every word was made up by somebody.

What is decisionism? It's the practice of persuading people to say certain things expressing a "decision for Christ" and basing their assurance of salvation on having said those things. If you ask someone who claims to be a Christian how he knows he is, he will usually say something about the occasion on which he prayed to receive Christ. That's fine. Unless that's the only evidence he has. The whole book of 1 John was written so we could be sure we are saved. It doesn't tell us to hark back to our "salvation experience," genuine though it may have been. Instead, John tells us to look at our *present* lives and look for evidence of salvation in the way we're living now. Such traits would include experiencing fellowship with God and other believers (1:6–7), the absence of practicing sin (though you will stumble and sin occasionally, you will hate it — 3:7–8), a reverence for God's commandments (3:23–24), a genuine love for others, especially fellow believers (4:7–11), and several other traits. Now look at the following statistics and see how modern evangelistic efforts seem to be producing such converts.

- An October 2003 survey conducted by the Barna Group found that 45% of those who profess to be born-again Christians believed that gambling was morally acceptable. 49% believed that "living with someone of the opposite sex without being married" was morally acceptable. Slightly less than half (49%) were comfortable with "enjoying sexual thoughts or fantasies about someone," while one-third of those professing to be born again thought that abortion was all right.

- In 2001, a survey conducted by the Alan Guttmacher Institute in New York found that "13 percent of abortion patients describe themselves as born-again or evangelical Christians."

- According to a *World Magazine* article entitled "Porn Nation," of the men belonging to the Christian organization Promise

Keepers (who make a promise to be "committed to practicing spiritual, moral, ethical, and sexual purity"), 53 percent visit porn sites weekly.

- A 2009 Barna Group study found that among individuals who describe themselves as Christian, close to half believe that Satan does not exist, two-fifths believe that they are not responsible to share their faith with others, one-third contend that Jesus sinned while He was on earth, and one-quarter do not believe that the Bible is accurate in all of its principles.

- 41 percent of self-proclaimed Christians believe that "the Bible, the Koran, and the Book of Mormon are all different expressions of the same spiritual truths" —- despite the books' radical differences on salvation, truth, and the nature of God.

- Only 46 percent of born-again adults believe in the existence of absolute moral truth.

- Pollster George Barna noted, "Although most Americans consider themselves to be Christian and say they know the content of the Bible, less than one out of ten Americans demonstrate such knowledge through their actions. With over 173 million Christians in the U.S., there are tens of millions who say that they love God and yet they are liars, thieves, fornicators, adulterers, and child-murderers."

- Despite 8 out of 10 teens describing themselves as Christian, 61 percent believe a place in heaven can be *earned* through good works; 63 percent believe Muslims, Buddhists, Christians, Jews, and all other people pray to the same God; and 58 percent believe all religious faiths teach equally valid truths.

- An "Ethics of American Youth Survey" found that in the prior 12 months, 74 percent of *Christian* teens cheated on a test, 93 percent lied to a parent, and 63 percent physically hurt someone when angered.

- The Barna Group also found that teens who profess to be born again and attend church regularly were just as likely as secular teens to engage in Internet theft of music and to illegally copy CDs (77 percent to 81 percent, respectively).

- In a joint statement, youth specialists Josh McDowell and Ron Luce made a sobering announcement: "Incredible as it may seem, 'accepting Christ' and making a profession of faith makes little to no difference in a young person's attitudes and behaviors. The majority of our churched young people are adopting 'a Christianity' but it is not true Christianity"; 98 percent of youth ministers and pastors McDowell surveyed agree with that assessment.

- In researching families in the U.S., the Southern Baptist Council on Family Life discovered a gut-wrenching statistic: "88 percent of the children raised in evangelical homes leave church at the age of 18, never to return." This mass exodus is seen not just among Southern Baptist churches, but across denominational lines.

- In the March/April 1993 issue of *American Horizon*, a major U.S. denomination disclosed that in 1991, 11,500 churches had obtained 294,784 decisions for Christ. Unfortunately, they could find only 14,337 in fellowship. Despite intense follow-up, they could not account for approximately 280,000 (95 percent) of their "converts." That's not at all unusual.

- After a recent evangelistic crusade, one church member stated, "Our church, which participated at every stage, received about 25 names for follow-up. These were mostly people in our area who did not identify with a church. We were instructed that many of these decisions might be fuzzy about what happened at the crusade and we should make sure they really understood the gospel. But we had cold receptions and not even enough interest to even begin the recommended Bible study class for new believers. To my knowledge, none of those 25 even visited our church after several contacts and pastoral visits."

In this same book, author Ray Comfort observes, "Paul's warning to Titus seems to be true of much of the modern Church: 'They profess to know God, but in works they deny Him' (Titus 1:16). Neither their beliefs nor their behavior aligns with biblical Christianity."

According to theologian A.W. Tozer, "It is my opinion that tens of thousands of people, if not millions, have been brought into some kind of religious experience by accepting Christ, and *they have not been saved.*"[5]

The late D. James Kennedy of Coral Ridge Ministries said, "The vast majority of people who are members of churches in America today are not Christians. I say that without the slightest fear of contradiction. I base it on empirical evidence of twenty-four years of examining thousands of people."[6]

Obviously, the Church in America is producing lots of "decisions," but only a tiny percentage of real Christians. What is wrong with our evangelism?

Ray Comfort and others believe that a major part of our approach is wrong. We're trying to be seeker-sensitive by thinking positively. We don't want to talk about nasty things like sin, judgment, damnation, and hell. We want to talk about grace, but not law. Yet the Bible tells us that the law is our "schoolmaster" to lead us to Christ (Gal. 3:24). The word schoolmaster is a poor translation. The Greek word actually used there refers to a specialized class of slave whose job it was to bring the child to the teacher and reinforce the teacher's lessons by making sure the child studied diligently. So the purpose of the law is not to save us, which only Christ can do, but to compel us to go to Him.

The modern method is to ignore the Law and just talk about grace. We are offering people salvation by grace when often their hearts have not been truly convicted of their awful sin by the Law. The result is that a lot of our converts are really only taking out what they think is fire insurance — a "Get Out of Jail Free" card to be kept as protection against hell. Without genuine conviction by the Law, they repeat words we suggest to them and trust in that brief ritual for salvation. No wonder so many of them can't be found in churches a few weeks or months later.

Ray Comfort says that we offer Jesus to people as a "life improver." We tell him that Christ will fix all their problems and make them happy. Some TV preachers even promise them wealth. Well, He certainly fixes a lot of problems. Countless lives have been transformed, marriages healed, addictions broken, and families reunited. But the Christian life is not one of unbroken bliss. The Apostle Paul expressed that the life of faith was no easy road. He related his own story of beatings, imprisonments, hunger, exposure, rejection, and a slew of other forms of persecutions. Jesus promised His followers that the world would hate them as it had hated Him. Some life improvement!

Ray likens Christ in our lives to a parachute. Wearing a parachute doesn't make a flight more pleasant; in fact, it adds to the already considerable discomfort of sitting in those miserable seats they put in airplanes. But the parachute becomes a treasure when we realize that the plane is going down and we are all going to have to jump out sooner or later.

Charles Finney, the leading evangelist of the Second Great Awakening, saw hundreds of thousands of people come to Jesus under his ministry in the 1800s. He was a strong advocate of presenting the Law to them to show them their utter depravity and sinfulness. A study was made 15 years after his ministry ended to see if his converts had been genuine. The study showed that 75 percent of them were still following Christ and active in local churches. Radically different from today's evangelism. Finney didn't ask people for "decisions." Rather, he preached the holy Law of God to them. Often, his hearers would be under such deep conviction that they would cry out for mercy from God, as did many who heard Whitefield, Wesley, and Jonathan Edwards during the First Great Awakening. Finney explained the need for true conviction in a letter titled *A Cause of Spurious Conversions*[7]:

> Pains enough had not been taken to search the heart and thoroughly detect and expose the sinner's depravity, so as to make him see the need of the gospel remedy. If I am not mistaken, there has been, in many cases, an error committed in urging sinners to submission before they are prepared to understand what true submission is . . . to believe, before they have understood their need of Christ; to resolve to serve God, before they have at all understood what the service of God is. . . .
>
> Consequently all his ideas of God, of sin, of his own guilt and desert of punishment, his need of a Saviour, the necessity of his being saved from his sins — in short, every fundamental idea of the Christian religion is apprehended by him with very little clearness. His mind is dark; his heart is hard. . . .
>
> In short, instead of seeing his necessities, his true character and relations, his views of all these things are so exceedingly superficial, that he has not apprehended and

does not apprehend, the necessity and nature of gospel salvation.

Even among those who profess Christ and join a church, the spiritual commitment level seems to be low. Our churches today are full of people whose lives reflect the world around them more than the teachings of Scripture. Ask any pastor what percentage of his congregation is truly walking with God on a daily basis and you'll find that the picture is not encouraging.

So the Church itself is a battlefield. The enemy has deceived many of us into believing that we need to offer people something better than what they have in order to get them to change. What we should be doing is showing them just how rotten what they already have is.

Seeker-Friendly

This brings me to my next bone of contention, the "seeker-friendly" or "seeker-sensitive" movement in the Church. The idea seems to be that we must make the unsaved comfortable in our church services in order to attract them to the Church and the gospel. If we make them like coming to church, they will keep coming and hearing the gospel. Hopefully, they will eventually respond and get saved.

The first problem with this is that God's plan for evangelism is not for the world to come into the Church, but for the Church to "Go into all the world and preach the gospel." That's from Mark 16:15. We're reversing the process when we try to get the world into the church. We can't get off the hook as easily as inviting people to church to hear the preacher. We're all supposed to be getting equipped for the work of the ministry in the Church and then going out to the world with the message of the gospel. Of course that's much more intimidating to most of us, so it's no wonder we count on the preacher to do all the preaching.

There's another problem. God doesn't want sinners to be comfortable in church. He wants them to be convicted. Check out 1 Corinthians 14:24–25:

> But if all prophesy, and an unbeliever or an ungifted man enters, he is convicted by all, he is called to account by all; the secrets of his heart are disclosed; and so he will fall on his face and worship God, declaring that God is certainly among you.

I've been under conviction plenty of times and I can tell you, it's anything but comfortable. I think what God is trying to say is that our church services should be so filled with a sense of God's holiness that unbelievers who may enter will be convicted of their sin. That's not going to happen very well if the believers look, act, and talk just like their godless neighbors. No difference, no conviction. And if we dumb down our music from that which exalts the majesty and beauty of God to contemporary stuff with high volume and low message content, we can't expect our unsaved visitors to see that we have a lot to offer them that they can't get from YouTube.

All this is not to say that unsaved visitors shouldn't be made to feel *welcome*. Of course they should know that they are welcome and loved in our gatherings. But feeling loved and feeling comfortable are two different things. They should feel loved because of our warm and accepting welcome. But they should feel convicted by our holy behavior, our beautiful, melodious music, and our solid, high-protein preaching.

I've been to "contemporary" church services. The effort to make the unsaved comfortable was painfully obvious. The music was trendy and rhythm driven, some of it boringly repetitive and most of it shallow in message content. Habits of dress tended to be very informal so that those who arrived in shorts and flip-flops would fit in. Sometimes even the preacher was dressed not just casually but apparently carelessly. The "worship" time was led by a team of professional-looking musicians, and their music was loud and dominated by beat, appealing to the body much more than challenging the spirit and intellect. The atmosphere in some of these churches is more similar to a rock concert than to a worship service.

I understand that the motive is pure in that they want to get the unsaved under the preaching of the gospel. What I'm taking issue with is the method. It seems to me that we're doing a much better job of bringing worldliness into the Church than taking the message of the Church into the world. Remember the difference between revival and apostasy?

Preaching

What's wrong with the country is what's wrong with the Church. And what's wrong with the Church is what's wrong with the pulpit. That's an oversimplification, but there's a lot of truth in it. Eventually, the beliefs, attitudes, and values that come through the preaching in the Church will be absorbed and lived out by most of the people of the Church. That's the way it's supposed to be, and that's why God puts such high requirements on preachers in 1 Timothy 3 and Titus 1.

I've heard some great preaching and teaching in church. I've also heard a wide variety of bad preaching and teaching. Some of it was hellfire-and-brimstone shouting that didn't have much Scripture mixed in with the message. Some of it was very academic, leaving me with the feeling that I had just heard something that I was supposed to remember, but for the life of me I couldn't see why I needed it. Some of it was presented well, but didn't address the crying needs of my heart.

We live in a day when Christians and non-Christians alike are desperately looking for answers. The Bible has those answers, and we need to understand them and express them to the people who need them in a way they will understand. That doesn't mean that we should let the audience decide what the preacher will preach. It means that the preachers and teachers in the Church had better be sensitive to the leading of God in what they say and how they say it. Something is wrong when people can attend church for years and never feel that God has spoken to them in a way that has changed them inside. Good doctrine is described in 1 Timothy 6:3:

> If anyone advocates a different doctrine and does not agree with sound words, those of our Lord Jesus Christ, and with the doctrine conforming to godliness.

Good preaching is that which agrees with the words of Jesus and the doctrine conforming to godliness. That means we should pay special attention to the words of Christ and that our preaching should be aimed at producing godly character growth in the listeners. Most preachers would agree that we have to be able to think rightly before we can live rightly. But it takes a very mature preacher to be able to preach Scripture in context and still make application that will produce spiritual growth. Some preachers sound like seminary professors, so academic that you listen to them and wonder why in the world you needed to know what was just said. If it's in the Bible, it must be important, but if it is, why didn't he tell me why? What am I supposed to do with the information? Just remember it? Will it be on a test or something?

Some preachers never get off first base. Every Sunday they preach a salvation message for the few unsaved people who might be present. Meanwhile, the true sheep go unfed. Of course they should read and study the Scripture on their own, but that kind of preaching won't encourage them to do so.

Some preachers only preach topically. They hit all their favorite topics and those that they perceive to be needed by their parishioners. That's fine as far as it goes, but we also need to approach the Bible in some organized way so that we get a clear sense of how it's organized and how it goes together.

It's ugly when preachers go too far the other way, though. I've read stuff from some preachers who think topical preaching is low-class stuff. Expositional is the only way to go. In fact one pastor said in a book he wrote that those who preach topically are just looking for proof texts for their pet theories. Pretty arrogant.

Another, a well-known radio Bible teacher, wrote a whole book on how to study the Bible without ever mentioning topical study. To me, that seems just plain dumb. There are times in life when we face issues and we need to know what God has to say about one specific problem. If I'm contemplating marriage, I'd better seek God's mind through study of marriage in the Scriptures. If my child has a life-threatening illness, I'll want to know about calling the elders for anointing and prayer. And I may not have time to search the Bible from Genesis 1:1 before finally arriving at James 5:14. If I'm deep in debt, I will need to find out what God says about finances. Note that Proverbs, which encourages us to seek wisdom like silver and gold, is not neatly laid out in themes. It's nuts and bolts, jumping from one topic to another much of the time.

Many of the great preachers of early America did a lot of preaching by topic. Read them and you will find sermons on everything from elections to war to politics to natural disasters to education. If it was in the papers, it was in the pulpit. Nowadays some preachers are so afraid of topical preaching that they ignore pressing issues that their people are responsible to deal with as citizens. We're losing our culture, yet many preachers stick to lofty theological concepts that great theologians have differed on for hundreds of years. Fiddling while Rome burns.

Whew. Glad I got that one off my chest.

Ultimately, it's not the method of preaching that matters nearly as much as the preacher's own spiritual condition. If he is walking closely and humbly with his God, the Lord can direct him in both preparation and presentation. God knows what the people of the church need to hear. So again we're reminded that everything rises and falls on leadership. What's wrong with the church is what's wrong with the pulpit.

Age Segregation

For at least as long as I can remember, churches have been following the example of schools in separating people from each other by age. When a church advertises itself as "family friendly" they mean that they have age-graded programs for every member of the family. Bring your family to us and we guarantee you won't see each other again until lunchtime. Church has become a place where we go to have our families divided. Some churches even divide adult Sunday school classes by gender so that husbands don't go to class with their wives. We have not only Sunday school classes for all ages of children, but children's church, too, so kids don't sit with their parents in the "adult" service. Teenagers usually attend the main service with adults, but cloister in their own little section of pews rather than sitting with their parents. I knew one church where a section was reserved for youth in order to keep them off the back row where they could get into mischief more easily.

This systematized segregation has its effects. Even during those events and times where age divisions are not enforced, there is little mingling between age groups. Adults hang with adults, teens with teens, kids with kids. Seldom do you see a teenager in an extended conversation with a middle-aged adult.

The age segregation these young people experience in school follows them into the life of the Church, where there is supposed to be a sense of family. But the family is divided and nobody seems to see it as a problem. Year after year we see another class of young people go off to college, seldom if ever to come back — either to the church or to their faith. We worry about this, but the only remedy usually suggested is "better youth programs." Nobody ever seems to wonder if perhaps the reason we're losing them is because we never built deep relationships between them and the older people of the church.

Rather than giving up and assuming that this is just the best we can do, the Church needs to take a multi-prong approach to the youth problem. First, we need to teach parents how to parent. If parents would see their responsibility to train their children rather than expecting the Church to do it in two or three hours per week, they would be open to getting some training in parenting. Further, we need to involve young people in the life of the Church much more fully. We need to make it a major tenet of our youth programs that young people need to know old people. We need to stop grouping kids together and entertaining them. Can't we see that it just doesn't work? It keeps kids away from the mature role models they need to learn from and isolates them from the real-world issues facing the Church. Young people should be involved in "adult" matters as early and as much as possible, both in the family and the Church. Kids who carry their own weight by taking responsibility grow up much faster than those who spend their youth being entertained. We need to find ways for young folks to perform functions in the church that are normally done by adults. They'll be slow to become adults if they never play the role.

Young people can sing, play musical instruments, give announcements, help with sound and other technical functions, pass offering plates, give congregational readings, welcome visitors, assist elderly and handicapped persons, carry umbrellas to arriving congregants in rainy weather, etc. They should do these things and more. And they should do them as individual church members, not always in groups of young people. Kids should be encouraged to "graduate" from the youth group and attend adult Sunday school classes and sit with their families in the main worship service. They will never get interested in adult issues until they have some in-depth exposure to adults.

If your church has all the age-segregated programs, just say no. Honor your father and mother by preferring to sit with them in church instead of with your buddies. Leave the teen Sunday school class and attend an adult class. Skip the childish youth activities and get involved in service projects with the adults of the church. When the youth pastor begs you to come back because the other kids need your more mature influence, offer to take some of them under your wing and take them along when you do adult things. It won't be easy to stand out, but that's what leaders are called to do.

I wish you knew my friend Jason. He is an 18-year-old man I know who has decided he'd rather grow up than wallow in the youth culture. He went to the youth group for a while and thought that it was fun, but he had better things to do with his time. Jason sits with his family in church while the other young folks sit whispering in their groups. They listen to rock, "Christian" or not, while Jason hones his considerable skills as a classic cellist. Other college kids are shaggy and tattooed; Jason is neatly barbered and in a suit. Jason is not arrogant, stiff, or formal. He is a fun guy with a good sense of humor and people of all ages like him just fine. But if you want to chat with him, choose a worthwhile subject because you'll never get him interested in the usual youth group gossip. Jason is one sharp guy and I respect him for being brave enough to be different. It will serve him well.

Endnotes

1. John Henry Thomas, Esq. and John Farquhar Fraser, Esq., *The Reports of Sr. Edward Coke, KNT in Six Volumes*, "Calvin's Case" (London: Joseph Butterworth & Son, 1826), Vol. 4, p. 6.

2. http://www.econlib.org/library/LFBooks/Burke/brkSWv3c3.html.

3. http://www.google.com/search?q=prefer+a+law+by+which+a+kingdom+hath+been+happily+governed&btnG=Search+Books&tbm=bks&tbo=1

4. Ray Comfort, *God Has a Wonderful Plan for Your Life: The Myth of the Modern Message* (Bellflower, CA: Living Waters Publications, 1999).

5. http://billsbible.blogspot.com/2010/03/13-evangelistic-phrases-that-produce.html.

6. http://webcache.googleusercontent.com/search?q=cache:ONcBFYAQHPcJ:www.jaywingard.com/2007/12/.

7. http://www.ccel.org/f/finney/fire/formats/fire.txt.

Chapter 11

THE COURTS

America was founded on the principle of government by the consent of the governed. That's a constitutional republic. The people elect representatives to make policy on their behalf. But for over half a century now, liberal elites have been frustrated in their efforts to convince the majority of their superior wisdom, which would dictate different outcomes in law and policy than would be chosen by the average unenlightened American. So, growing impatient, the elites have turned to the judiciary to get the results they have failed to get through legislation. Their main attack on the majority's will these days is through the court system, and their champions are liberal judges who are willing to rule contrary to the intent of the Constitution. They believe their wisdom is superior to that of the founders who wrote it.

One such liberal icon is Supreme Court Justice John Paul Stevens, retired. He was interviewed on CBS's *60 Minutes* on November 28,

2010. It was a completely one-sided interview, with reporter Scott Pelley throwing softball questions to the judge. He was especially gushy over Stevens' public suggestion that President George W. Bush was a tyrant. Pelley praised Stevens, saying that he had "shaped more American history than any Supreme Court justice alive." He was impressed with the justice's opinions on the rights of terrorist suspects and called them "among the most important of his career."

Not to be outdone, National Public (government-controlled) Radio honored ultraliberal Justice William Brennan that same weekend. Legal correspondent Nina Totenberg quoted the conservative magazine *National Review* as saying that no individual "on or off the court" had had a more profound impact on America than Brennan. She forgot to mention that the *Review* article had expressed revulsion that a judge could have so much effect on public policy.

Well, it's cause for revulsion. For a long time, but much more frequently in recent years, judges and courts have acted unconstitutionally to reverse the decisions of the citizens and their elected representatives. Look at some examples.

In 1875 Congress passed a law banning all racial segregation. But in 1882 the Supreme Court struck down the law. It wasn't until 1954 in Brown v. Board of Education that the Court reversed itself. The Court had preserved segregation 70 years after Congress had outlawed it through the democratic process.

In the year 2000, the voters of California passed Proposition 22, which declared that marriage is only between one man and one woman. A state judge struck Prop. 22 down in a 2002 decision. Do you see what that one man did? He used his position to take the definition of marriage out of the hands of the majority of voters and usurp it for himself. The same thing happened as judges in Massachusetts, Vermont, and Hawaii did likewise.

The Nevada Constitution requires a two-thirds majority vote in the legislature to authorize a tax increase. But the Nevada Supreme Court ordered that clause of the Constitution to be ignored and instead directed a tax increase to boost spending on education. Can you believe this? The state court ruled that part of the Constitution is constitutional. Brilliant.

The Kansas legislature, listening to the voice of the people, passed a death penalty statute. The Kansas Supreme Court struck it down. The same court ruled that additional funding must be given to the state department of education or the court would take control of education spending. This, despite the fact that the state's Constitution requires that all spending originate and reside solely in the legislature.

In New Jersey, a 2002 candidate for U.S. Senate dropped out of the race because he felt he was too far behind in the polls to catch up. He quit 35 days before the election. His party, unwilling to let the seat go without a fight, wanted to place another candidate on the ballot. But by state law, a candidate could be replaced by another name only if the "vacancy shall occur not later than the 51st day before the general election." That's pretty clear, but the court ignored the law and ordered a new name to be placed on the ballot. The new candidate won the race. Because the court broke the law in order to advance a political agenda, his party won a U.S. Senate seat they would otherwise have lost.

In the hotly contested race between Bush and Gore for President in 2000, the Florida Supreme Court took matters into their own hands. The state law said quite clearly that all election vote tallies were to be submitted to the Secretary of State's office by 5 p.m. on the 7th day following the election. By law, all results turned in after that time were to be ignored. Yet those judges ruled that 5 p.m.

on the 7th day really meant 5 p.m. on the 19th day, and that the word "ignored" didn't really mean "ignored." Instead, the Secretary of State must accept all results, even those that did not comply with the law. Uh . . . isn't that just the opposite of what the law said?

Those are some examples of state courts stealing authority from state legislatures and the voters who elect them. On the national front, the Supreme Court has repeatedly ignored the clear intent of the Constitution and the will of the majority. Perhaps their most infamous decision was the 1973 Roe v. Wade ruling that has resulted in the legalized murder of 50 million American babies. The majority decision spoke of "emanations" and "penumbras" seeping out of the Constitution (where the rest of us would see only words). What they meant was they knew what the writers of the Constitution — Madison and others — really meant. Never mind that no other Supreme Court in our 200 years of existence had ever noticed these emanations and penumbras. Never mind that none of the founders' writings mentioned them. The 1973 Supreme Court knew more about the meaning of the Constitution than did those who wrote it or those who had applied it in court for two centuries. They discovered a "right to privacy" that Madison had no idea he wrote into the document.

Here is where we need to discuss the term *judicial activism*. There is nothing wrong with activism. I am an activist and I hope you are, too. But it's something no judge has a right to do from the bench. The examples above were all of judicial activism. It means the act of doing what a judge wants to do instead of what the law requires.

A judge's job is not to *interpret* the law, but to *apply* the law. He is supposed to rule according to *original intent*. That is, what the writers of the law and the legislators who voted on it intended. He is not to *interpret* the law to mean what he wants it to mean in order to excuse his ruling the way he wants to rule. The Constitution is supposed to be the final authority in all courts. And that means what the framers of the Constitution intended by what they said. For a modern court to twist what the framers said in order to rule as they want to rule is judicial activism. It's often referred to as "legislating from the bench." It's entirely illegal, wrong, and unwise.

We have a great Constitution. It established a form of government that has lasted over 200 years while most other countries have gone through several constitutions. It contains provisions to make changes in it when needed, and that process is called amendment. It is such a good document that it has been amended only 27 times in all our history. It is intentionally hard to amend, requiring two-thirds approval of all the states. That's as it should be. It would destroy the stability of our country for it to be changeable by a whim. Unfortunately, the Supreme Court and lower courts routinely "change" it by interpreting it the way they choose rather than reading it as the framers intended. The Constitution is an excellent guarantee of our freedoms, but when the courts choose to "interpret" rather than apply it, our freedoms are blowing in the wind.

About half the judges in our country are elected, the other half are appointed by some official person or body. Bad judges who are elected should be voted out. Appointed judges who rule unconstitutionally should be impeached. The common belief is that appointed judges are "appointed for life." That's not true. The Constitution says they are appointed for "the duration of good behavior." Judges, even federal judges, have been and still can be impeached. Some should be.

When Jimmy Carter was president, he not only appointed liberal judges to open positions, he went a giant step further. He created over 400 new judgeships and filled them with liberal judges, too. In one four-year presidential term, we were saddled with 400 new activist judges. One more reason to elect good presidents.

The reason that judges legislate from the bench and that the public tolerates it is that we don't understand our own Constitution. Though it's a short document, most of us have never read it. Most law schools don't teach it, even though it's the basis of all our law. Our attitude toward the Constitution, our laws, and our courts is all wrong. We're indebted to David Barton of Wallbuilders for researching this in the writings of our founders and explaining it so that we can correct the problems and get our freedom and national stability back. I've drawn the following points from his article titled *Five Judicial Myths* from his website, www.Wallbuilders.com. Please read the entire article on his site. He has each point greatly expanded and thoroughly footnoted to verify his sources.

Answers to the Five Judicial Myths

1. THE JUDICIARY IS NOT A CO-EQUAL BRANCH OF GOVERNMENT, ALONG WITH THE LEGISLATIVE AND THE EXECUTIVE.

Federalist #78: "The judiciary, on the contrary, has no influence over either the sword or the purse; no direction either of the strength or of the wealth of the society; and can take no active resolution whatever. It may truly be said to have neither force nor will. . . . The judiciary, from the nature of its functions, will always be the least dangerous to the political rights of the Constitution. . . . [T]he judiciary is, beyond comparison, the weakest of the three departments of power. . . . [And] the general liberty of the people can never be endangered from that quarter."

E. William Giles, member of the first federal Congress under the Constitution: "Is [the Judiciary department] formed by the

Constitution? It is not. . . . It is only declared that there shall be such a department, and it is directed to be formed by the two other departments, who owe a responsibility to the people. . . . The number of judges, the assignation of duties, the fixing of compensations, the fixing the times when, and the places where, the courts shall exercise the functions, etc., are left to the entire discretion of Congress. The spirit as well as the words of the Constitution are completely satisfied, provided one Supreme Court be established. . . . Congress may postpone the sessions of the courts for eight or ten years, and establish others to whom they could transfer all the powers of the existing courts."

As Rep. Steve King correctly explains, "Constitutionally, Congress can reduce the Supreme Court to nothing more than Chief Justice Roberts sitting at a card table with a candle" — a power that the judiciary cannot reciprocally exercise over Congress.

2. THE JUDICIARY IS NOT TO BE AN INDEPENDENT BRANCH OF GOVERNMENT

A. John Dickinson, signer of the Constitution: "[W]hat innumerable acts of injustice may be committed — and how fatally may the principles of liberty be sapped — by a succession of judges utterly independent of the people?"

B. Thomas Jefferson: "It should be remembered as an axiom of eternal truth in politics that whatever power in any government is independent is absolute also. . . . Independence can be trusted nowhere but with the people in mass."

D. Jonathan Mason, law student trained by John Adams and an early member of Congress: "The independence of the judiciary so much desired will — if tolerated — soon become something like supremacy. They will, indeed, form the main pillar of this goodly fabric; they will soon become the only remaining pillar, and they will presently be so strong as to crush and absorb the others into their solid mass."

E. Thomas Jefferson: "We think, in America, that it is necessary to introduce the people into every department of government. . . . Were I called upon to decide whether the people had best be omitted in the legislative or judiciary department, I would say it is better to leave them out of the legislative. The execution of the laws is more important than the making them."

F. Joseph Nicholson, early member of Congress, successfully managed the impeachment of multiple early federal judges: "Give [judges] the powers and the independence now contended for and . . . your government becomes a despotism and they become your rulers. They are to decide upon the lives, the liberties, and the property of your citizens; they have an absolute veto upon your laws by declaring them null and void at pleasure; they are to introduce at will the laws of a foreign country . . . after being clothed with this arbitrary power, they are beyond the control of the nation. . . . If all this be true — if this doctrine be established in the extent which is now contended for — the Constitution is not worth the time we are now spending on it. It is — as it has been called by its enemies — mere parchment. For these judges, thus rendered omnipotent, may overleap the Constitution and trample on your laws."

3. THE JUDICIARY IS NOT THE SOLE BRANCH OF GOVERNMENT CAPABLE OF DETERMINING CONSTITUTIONALITY

James Madison: "But the great objection . . . is that the Legislature itself has no right to expound the Constitution — that wherever its meaning is doubtful, you must leave it to take its course until the Judiciary is called upon to declare its meaning. . . . I beg to know upon what principle it can be contended that any one department draws from the Constitution greater powers than another in marking out the limits.

Luther Martin, framer of the Constitution and attorney general of Maryland: "A knowledge of mankind and of legislative affairs cannot be presumed to belong in a higher degree to the Judges than to the Legislature."

John Randolph of Roanoke: "[I]f you pass the law, the judges are to put their veto upon it by declaring it unconstitutional. Here is a new power of a dangerous and uncontrollable nature contended for. . . . The power which has the right of passing — without appeal — on the validity of laws is your sovereign."

Thomas Jefferson: "[O]ur Constitution . . . has given — according to this opinion — to one of [the three branches] alone the right to prescribe rules for the government of the others — and to that one, too, which is unelected by and independent of the nation. . . . The Constitution, on this hypothesis, is a mere thing of wax in the hands of the Judiciary which they may twist and shape into any form they please."

Rufus King, signer of the Constitution, framer of the Bill of Rights: "The judges must interpret the laws; they ought not to be legislators."

Thomas Jefferson: "[T]he opinion which gives to the judges the right to decide what laws are constitutional and what not, not only for themselves in their own sphere of action, but for the Legislature and Executive also in their spheres, would make the Judiciary a despotic branch."

James Madison: "[R]efusing or not refusing to execute a law, to stamp it with its final character . . . makes the Judiciary department paramount in fact to the Legislature, which was never intended and can never be proper."

Thomas Jefferson: "You seem . . . to consider the judges as the ultimate arbiters of all constitutional questions — a very dangerous doctrine indeed, and one which would place us under the despotism of an oligarchy. Our judges are as honest as other men and not more so. They have, with others, the same passions for party, for power, and the privilege of their corps. . . . [A]nd their power the more dangerous as they are in office for life and not responsible, as the other functionaries are, to the elective.

President Andrew Jackson: "Each public officer who takes an oath to support the Constitution swears that he will support it as he understands it, and not as it is understood by others. . . . The authority of the Supreme Court must not, therefore, be permitted to control the Congress or the Executive.

4. FEDERAL JUDGES DO NOT HOLD LIFETIME APPOINTMENTS

The Constitution says that judges hold their office only during "good behavior" (Art. III, Sec. 1).

Federal judges may be removed by Congress for misbehavior, which, historically, did not include only criminal behavior but also other misbehavior.

Historically, federal judges have been removed from the bench by Congress for contradicting an order of Congress, for profanity, for rude treatment of witness in a courtroom, for drunkenness, for judicial high-handedness and a variety of other reasons.

The Constitution provides six clauses on impeachment — the most often-mentioned subject in the Constitution.

Alexander Hamilton: "the abuse or violation of some public trust . . . [or for] injuries done immediately to the society itself."

William Rawle, legal authority and author of early constitutional commentary: "the inordinate extension of power, the influence of party and of prejudice as well as attempts to 'infringe the rights of the people.' "

Justice Joseph Story, a "Father of American Jurisprudence" appointed to the Supreme Court by President James Madison: "unconstitutional opinions" and "attempts to subvert the fundamental laws and introduce arbitrary power."

5. THE PURPOSE OF THE SUPREME COURT IS NOT TO PROTECT THE MINORITY FROM THE MAJORITY, AND CONGRESS IS A BETTER PROTECTOR OF MINORITY RIGHTS THAN IS THE JUDICIARY

A. George Washington: "[T]he fundamental principle of our Constitution . . . enjoins [requires] that the will of the majority shall prevail."

B. Thomas Jefferson: "[T]he will of the majority [is] the natural law of every society [and] is the only sure guardian of the rights of man. Perhaps even this may sometimes err. But its errors are honest, solitary, and short-lived."

C. The Judiciary is now regularly anti-majoritarian.

D. The primary purpose of the Supreme Court is not to protect the minority from the majority.

E. The primary purpose of the Bill of Rights is not to protect the minority from the majority; the purpose of the Bill of Rights is to protect every citizen, whether in the minority or the majority, from the intrusion upon their rights by government.

F. Congress is a better guardian of the people and the minority than are the courts.

Thomas Jefferson: "When the Legislative or Executive functionaries act unconstitutionally, they are responsible to the people in their elective capacity. The exemption of the judges from that is quite dangerous enough. I know no safe depository of the ultimate powers of the society but the people themselves; and if we think them [the people] not enlightened enough to exercise their control with a wholesome discretion, the remedy is not to take it from them, but to inform their discretion by education. This is the true corrective of abuses of constitutional power.

We could go on and on about abuses of judicial power, but they're so common that we really don't need a lot of proof that the judiciary is far out of hand. What we need to do is to recognize what the root of all the abuse is. It is a broadly accepted but wrong view of the powers of the courts.

If God calls you to fight His battles in the courts, you will quickly get acquainted with an organization known as the American Civil Liberties Union. The ACLU, founded in 1920 by Communist Roger Baldwin and others, seems dedicated to opposing what God supports and supporting what God opposes. The following points are taken from their website, www.ACLU.org.

On Criminal Justice

The ACLU opposes
- laws restricting areas where the sexual offenders of children can live;
- life sentences for juveniles convicted of extremely violent crimes;
- the "Three Strikes" law mandating harsher sentences for those with three felony convictions;
- withholding voting rights for felons.

The ACLU opposes the death penalty, and
- claims: "The death penalty is contrary to fundamental notions of human rights. The United States is the only

major country of the Western world that tolerates the death penalty";

- seeks to halt death penalty executions, claiming that "death by lethal injection is extraordinarily painful and [can] constitute cruel and unusual punishment."

On Illegal Drugs

The ACLU opposes

- mandatory sentencing laws for crack-cocaine possession;
- drug testing of welfare recipients;
- federal faith-based drug treatment programs;
- federal laws banning student loans to convicted drug addicts.

On Abortion:

The ACLU supports

- abortion and abortion-on-demand;
- increased funding for pro-abortion groups such as Planned Parenthood;
- Euthanasia.

The ACLU opposes

- abstinence-only sex education for students;
- conscience protection rights for medical providers;
- informed consent and "Women's Right to Know" laws;
- pro-life state license plates.

On Immigration & Illegal Aliens

The ACLU supports

- government services for illegal aliens.

The ACLU opposes

- federal immigration laws targeting border security and preventing entrance of illegal aliens as well as the enforcement of those laws;

- denying driver's licenses to illegal aliens;
- federal laws identifying citizenship status of those receiving treatment at medical facilities.

On Homosexual Issues

The ACLU supports

- gay marriage and benefits for gay "families";
- adoptions by gays, gays as foster parents, "parental" rights for gay "parents," and gay parent family training;
- gay clubs on school campuses, gay campus publications and articles on campus, and forcing straight students to attend gay sensitivity training;
- gays in the military;
- pro-gay state license plates.

The ACLU opposes

- marriage between only a man and a woman;
- a school competition asking "students to explain why preserving marriage between men and women is vital to society and why unborn children merit respect and protection."

The ACLU supports

- bigamy and polygamy;
- pedophilia and legalizing sex between children and adults;
- transgender rights.

Religious Expression Issues

The ACLU opposes

- Ten Commandments displays;
- religious symbols in public parks;
- prayers at military academies.

At the federal level, the ACLU opposes

- keeping "under God" in the Pledge of Allegiance;
- keeping the national motto ("In God We Trust") on currency;
- faith-based programs;
- the observance of religious holidays.

At the state level, the ACLU opposes

- the mention of God in a state motto;
- prayers to open legislatures;
- moment-of-silence laws at schools;
- educational choice and vouchers;
- prayer in judicial arenas.

At the local level, the ACLU opposes

- mayor's prayer breakfasts;
- city council prayers;
- school board prayers;
- nativity scenes on city property;
- religious symbols in city seals;
- voluntary distribution of Gideon Bibles.

In schools, the ACLU opposes

- graduation prayers;
- athletic prayers;
- intelligent design or any mention of creation or a Creator;
- prayers at school or at school events;
- school choirs singing religious songs.

Miscellaneous Issues

- Opposes library policies blocking access of minors to sexual content, gambling, and illegal activities;
- opposes denying visas to foreigners who oppose the United States government;

- opposes one federal agency from sharing with another federal agency the information that it has on Arabs in America;
- supports anti-American foreign terrorists captured on the battlefield having the same constitutional protections as U.S. citizens, even though the guarantees in the U.S. Constitution apply only to American citizens;
- supports activists disrupting military funerals and confronting the distraught family members with offensive and inappropriate language;
- opposes banning convicted sex offenders from having access to parks where children play;
- supports the notion that the "separation of church and state" trumps students' freedom of speech.

As you follow the news media, you will repeatedly hear about the ACLU's involvement in this or that legal case that is currently working its way through the courts. Although they take a few token cases supporting conservative causes, this is only a smokescreen. About 99 percent of the time, the ACLU is fighting ferociously for the wrong cause. You need to know about them because they have become the most powerful single group opposing righteousness in the judicial system. As a part of educating yourself about the workings of the court system, pay close attention to what the ACLU is up to.

Thankfully, God has raised up some Christian legal groups that are finally having some good success in reversing the influence of the ACLU. The American Center for Law and Justice (ACLJ) is led by attorney Jay Sekulow. Jay has been before the Supreme Court at least ten times and has won every case there so far. The Alliance Defense Fund is another group worthy of your support. Pray for these groups and support them financially if you can. They're fighting for you.

There are other things you can do as a citizen. In Iowa, the state supreme court ruled that the state could not outlaw gay "marriage." These justices thought their "lifetime" appointments would protect them from the wrath of the people. Oh, they knew that retention votes — votes on whether to keep a certain judge in office — are taken every so often. But they also knew that 99 percent of the time, the judge is retained. Surprise, surprise. When three of those justices came up for a retention vote in 2010, all three got booted out.

There are ways to get rid of bad judges. Elected ones can be voted out and appointed ones can be impeached. All it takes is a few determined people who will get others riled up.

Some of you need to go to law school and prepare to fight God's battles in the courtroom. Eventually, some of you will become judges as well. Wouldn't it be great if Christian homeschool grads were as dominant in the Supreme Court's makeup as Harvard is now? And all of us need to pray. God is the Author of law and He will give final justice.

Chapter 12

WHERE DO I START?

I t seems providential that I'm writing the last chapter of this book right now. It is Monday, May 2, 2011, and just hours since we heard the news that American forces in Pakistan yesterday attacked and killed terrorist mastermind Osama bin Laden. It's a solemn day for Americans who well remember September 11, 2001, when the Twin Towers in New York were blasted into history, along with 3,000 innocent lives, by hijacked passenger jets.

College students in Washington, DC, swarmed to the area outside the White House and spent the night in jubilant celebration, waving American flags and singing "The Star-Spangled Banner" over and over again. At Ground Zero (the site in New York City where the Twin Towers stood and which has now been turned into a memorial) another huge crowd gathered to celebrate the death of the man who planned the attack. No doubt bin Laden's death is a blow to international terrorism and ultimately saved many lives. But nobody seems to have any illusions that terrorism died with this one man. The sober reality is that the war will go on.

And our struggle goes on as well: the fight for the soul of America. For our greatest enemies are not in Pakistan or Afghanistan or Iraq or Iran. They are embedded in our own society, even in our own hearts. The battle is more than anything else a spiritual one, raging in the heavenlies. We fight in the physical world and in the unseen world as well. And Jesus is Lord of both.

So, having read the challenge in the preceding chapters, you face the issue of where to take your place in the army of God. What now?

The first thing is to pray. I know that sounds trite, because you're supposed to be doing that all the time. But I hope that after reading this book you have a clearer focus of how to pray. If I've been successful in writing it, you are convinced that you must do something and you have some idea of what that something is. Now you need to ask God to give you a vision for your immediate future, or fine tune it if you already have one. Saturate your mind with the Scriptures and spend serious time crying out to God for direction.

He may start you on one battlefield, say, pro-life work. Later He may reassign you to major on evangelism or politics or education. It's fun to speculate on where you may be 20 years from now and certainly you should think long term, but don't get distracted from the good you can do right now. Do something.

The second thing you should do is get your parents' counsel on this. This is critically important. You do not exist in a vacuum. You are not the Lone Ranger, you're a member of a family. You have been given your specific parents for a reason. God knows the reason, so don't worry about that. Just stay under your parents' authority and counsel and trust God that He can move their hearts in the right direction. Their love for you and their greater life experience are solid gold to you. Hopefully, they'll be excited that you're wanting to do something important with your time. If you have an idea for a mission and they feel some hesitations, listen to them. Maybe they're thinking of a different mission that would be more appropriate for your life right now. God may be showing them something you're missing. After all, they know you pretty well.

When they give you clearance to move ahead with something, get them involved with you as much as they can spare the time. You need their input along the way, as well as at the starting line. Involve your brothers and sisters, too, if possible. This must be a family movement if we want to save America. Remember, in Nehemiah they fought as families.

Third, get the counsel and support of your local church authorities. I hope they're already committed to the culture war. But if not, the reproof of seeing a young person passionate about it may be the jolt they need to see what's happening to our society. Pray for your pastor and elders, too. The local church is Christ's chosen body, remember. It's against the *Church* that the gates of hell cannot stand.

Speaking of the Church, it contains what I call the secret weapon of the young culture warrior. Care to guess what that is? Okay, I'll tell you. The secret weapon of young people is (drum roll, please) *old people.*

Uh . . . say what?

I said old people. Here's how it works. Say you're 15 and you want to do something significant for God. Maybe your objective is to rebuild the front porch for an elderly lady who can't afford to have the work done. You figure it's a chance to honor the gray head as Scripture commands, and hopefully get some gospel tracts to the neighborhood as well. But Mrs. Jones lives several miles away, and you can't drive yet. You also don't know beans about carpentry. You also don't have the bucks to purchase materials.

But you know Mr. Black from church. He's retired and he's something of a handy man. He's helped with some remodeling at church a time or two. So you ask your parents about it and they say yeah. He might be interested. So you mention it to Mr. Black, and what will he say? Will he say, "Look, I'm enjoying my retirement and I'm not about to give up my golf game so some starry-eyed 15 year old can fulfill a silly daydream"?

Not a chance. Mr. Black is going to be very interested, for several reasons. One, he will have finally met a young person who cares about doing something for somebody else. Two, most older people are lonely and bored and looking for friends and something good to do with their time now that they're not working. Three, most of them want to do something for ministry but need some ideas. Most people are short on initiative, remember.

So Mr. Black is in for the project. And if you treat him with respect, probably for future exploits, too. He'll supply the transportation and chip in a few bucks for lumber. Now you get your dad if he has time, a couple of your siblings and a few friends, some young people, and some adults. You collect the tools, make up your material list, scratch some more money together, and buy your stuff. Then you rebuild that porch, make a lifetime friend of Mrs. Jones, and hand out gospel tracts to the neighborhood when people ask why you're doing what you're doing. Maybe you've got some friends who don't like to hammer nails, so you get them to make some candy and give it out along with tracts to the neighborhood kids.

While all this has been developing, you've enlisted several people at church for a prayer team. Ask them to pray daily, and especially on the Saturday (or Saturdays) when you'll be on-site with the project. Keep a list of their names for prayer support with the next project also, and the list will grow over time. The more Ezras praying for the Nehemiahs, the more effective you will be. It's a local church thing.

The same principles will work in reforming your political party, starting a letters-to-the-editor campaign, or whatever. You need help from all ages, but older people are your nuclear arsenal.

Fourth, try some things. Life is a buffet, and you may sample a lot of dishes before you find that one entrée that makes you drool uncontrollably. You probably have talents in a number of different areas, and if you want to be a whole person you should use them all in proportion. But the thing that will keep you going when you run into difficulties — which you definitely will — is the thing that excites your innermost soul and sets you aflame with passion. God may give you a different passion 20 years from now, or He may not. Ask Him to give you a burning passion for the battle He wants you in now.

Fifth, read. Inform yourself about the different battlefields I've talked about in this book. You'll discover some other ones as well, because the enemy is active everywhere. You need to be learning all the time. As you read, one source will lead you to another and you will keep learning new stuff for the rest of your life. You will also become a more capable warrior.

Sixth, learn from your experiences. You can do this one of two ways: you can take part in a ministry project that somebody else starts, or you can start a project of your own, like Mrs. Jones's porch. You don't have to make a long-term commitment to take part in most ministries; just try it a time or two and see how you fit. You may work in an existing ministry for a while, get some experience, and come up with an idea for a ministry project of your own. You can get valuable experience either way.

And, one very important point. *Don't be afraid to fail.* The road to success is paved with lessons learned from failure. If you try an exploit and it doesn't work, don't throw in the towel. Analyze it to see what went wrong. Maybe you didn't do your homework first and went into it underprepared. Maybe you didn't have enough prayer support. Maybe some friends promised to help and copped out at the last minute. Figure out what went wrong and prepare in advance for it next time. But don't ever give up on doing works for God. Instead start small, learn from both success and failure, and build up as time goes on. Never think about giving up. "Quit" is just another four-letter word. It doesn't belong in a Christian's vocabulary.

Before we part company, I want to remind you of something very important: You are not alone. The task ahead of us is huge. Gigantic. But God is raising up an army of millions to deal with it. Many churches and other organizations are already doing great work in the culture war. Some of them will teach you important information for your own battles. Some of them deserve your support in theirs. As in Nehemiah, we're working on different sections of the wall, but it's all the same wall. You are part of God's answer for the problems of the world, but you don't have to be the whole answer. God has it covered. Be hopeful

Keep in mind also that the homeschooling movement is a moving of God. It was virtually nothing when my family started, and today it's estimated there are three million kids being taught at home. The hearts of the fathers are turning to the children and vice versa. Malachi chapter 4 says that's the key to forestalling God's curse on the land. Amen. If this book accomplishes what I hope it will, young people like you all over the country will get connected with each other and your families will join together to accomplish missions for God. Wouldn't it be exciting to attend *Take Back the Land* conferences and meet like-minded young people and their families, building networks and rebuilding America together? Stay in touch through our website, www.thelearningparent.com, and we'll keep you informed of what we're doing and what we see going on around the country.

Thanks for reading. I can't wait to see what our great God will accomplish through you in the days ahead. Now I leave you with a story.

If you've heard of the movie *Black Hawk Down,* you may know about the Battle of Mogadishu, Somalia. It was fought on October 3 and 4, 1993. I heard the story from General Jerry Boykin, the commander of ground forces for the operation. The objective of the mission was to capture some high henchmen of Somali terrorist warlord Mohamed Farrah Aidid. During the mission, an Army Black Hawk helicopter was shot down by a rocket. General Boykin mobilized every soldier available and sent in a rescue mission to save the surviving crew members. A half hour later and 1,800 meters away, another Black Hawk fell victim to rocket fire and went down with a crew of four aboard.

General Boykin was between a rock and a hard place. He had sent all available personnel to rescue the crew of the first chopper and they were fully committed as they fought their way through the blockaded streets of the city. The only supporting fire for the crew of the second helicopter was coming from two Army snipers in another chopper circling above the crash site. These two young men, Specialist First Class Randy Shughart and Master Sergeant Gary Gordon, could see movement inside the downed chopper and so knew that at least some of the crew were still alive. They radioed in to General Boykin for permission to land and take a position at the crash site to defend their buddies. "Put us in!" they begged.

General Boykin replied, "Guys, I can't. I've sent everything I've got to the other crash site. I can't support you."

Shughart and Gordon called in again a few minutes later. "Sir, the Somalis are coming from everywhere. We can't hold 'em off much longer. Please put us in!"

The general, his heart in his throat, said, "Guys, I can't. I'm trying my best to scrape together some support but it's going to take some time. Use your door guns, do whatever you can. I'll send you some help just as soon as I possibly can." He knew he had probably already lost four good men, and he couldn't stand the thought of sending these two heroic young guys down to be overwhelmed and killed with them.

But a few minutes later they were on the radio again. "Sir, they're coming too fast! We can't hold 'em off from up here. Our guys are alive down there and their only chance is for us to go in with them. Please put us in!" He could hear the desperation in the appeal.

General Boykin felt torn in half. He knew full well what these young men faced if they hit the ground. He also felt their agony at being held back from laying it all on the line for their comrades. With a breaking heart he finally said, "All right, guys. Go."

Gordon and Shughart went. Their Black Hawk descended through a hail of small arms fire and the two heroes jumped out, carrying their weapons and every round of ammunition they had. As the chopper rose once again they fought their way to the downed helicopter and slaughtered attacking Somali militiamen until they were finally overwhelmed by sheer numbers.

"Greater love has no one than this, that one lay down his life for his friends" (John 15:13). Gordon and Shughart were posthumously awarded the Medal of Honor.

What do you see as you look around you? Do you see the car-
nage and destruction the forces of Satan are creating every day? Do
you see masses of people living and dying and never hearing the
gospel of Christ? Do you hear the cry of millions of children growing up in homes where strife and bitterness color every moment of
the day? Do you see the loneliness of the elderly, locked into nursing homes and forgotten by their children? Do you see the steady
erosion of all that's beautiful about America — the best, most free,
most just, most blessed nation ever to adorn the face of God's green
earth?

You have a choice to make. You can say, "Ho hum. That's a
shame." Or you can say, "Put me in!"

Joshua's generation looked across the Jordan and saw enemy
forces entrenched in God's territory. They crossed the river, shouting by their actions, "Put us in!"

We really don't need another order. Our Commander has already said, "Go ye into all the world." Your response is up to you.

The Moses generation is watching you, Joshua.

Take back the land.

Master
Books®

Connect with Master Books®

masterbooks.net

An Imprint of New Leaf Publishing Group

facebook.com/**masterbooks**
twitter.com/**masterbooks4u**
youtube.com/**nlpgvideo**

nlpgblogs.com
nlpgvideos.com

Connect with Rick Boyer

facebook.com/**rickboyerusa**

thelearningparent.com
takebacktheland.com

*If you enjoyed the book, please write a review at Amazon.com, Christianbook.com, and other online review sites.

FOR YOU THEY SIGNED
by Marilyn Boyer

They risked everything so we could be free!

In 1776, 56 men signed their names on a document that they knew might well mean their certain deaths as traitors of the British Empire. The Declaration of Independence was a powerful statement of freedom, and this text will help you value those freedoms these men fought for in an insightfully fresh way. Historical revisionists have distorted or attempted to wipe away every trace of America's Christian heritage. *For You They Signed* provides an abundance of resources within one volume, including

- A full year of life-changing family or group devotional character studies

- Over 90 illustrations, biographical summaries, and insightful quotes

- Character quality definitions, Patrick Henry's speech delivered to the signers, the Christian nature of state constitutions, and the Christian nature of America's universities.

For You They Signed will help you catch the God-given vision of the founding fathers and let it ignite a fire for your family, community, and the generations to come.

ISBN: 978-0-89051-598-3

casebound • 400 pages • 8-1/2 x 11 • $34.99

Available at Christian bookstores nationwide or at www.nlpg.com